PRAIS

"I can't say enough good things about Rich Wilkerson, Jr. Not only is he a close friend and an incredible pastor, he is a compelling voice in this generation. His passion and insight shine clearly in *Sandcastle Kings*. It is human nature to want to build something that lasts; to make our lives count; to leave a legacy that goes beyond ourselves. Yet too often, we find ourselves dazzled and distracted by pursuits we know will never stand the test of time. In this book, Rich reveals the answer to our dilemma by focusing on the one who will never fade or wash away: Jesus."

—JUDAH SMITH, LEAD PASTOR, THE CITY CHURCH,
SEATTLE, WASHINGTON; AND *NEW YORK TIMES*
BESTSELLING AUTHOR OF *JESUS IS _____*.

"Thank you, Rich, for revealing this truth that we are all sandcastle kings. This book is a powerful reminder that God is our one true source for solid ground. While material things crumble away, God's firm foundation remains! It's time for us to drop our shovels and allow Jesus to take over."

—CHRISTINE CAINE, FOUNDER OF A21
CAMPAIGN AND PROPEL WOMEN

"Pastor Rich is one of those rare people who always lights up the room and makes everyone feel like a priority. His optimistic advice and his passion for the Word of God are contagious. He has had such a positive and enlightening influence on my family; we are so blessed to call him our pastor and our friend."

—KIM KARDASHIAN WEST

"Rich Wilkerson, Jr., is a gift to this generation. His enthusiasm for life, his rich family heritage in the church, and anointing to communicate the Word of God in a relevant, accessible, and approachable way, has and will continue to impact countless lives."

—BRIAN HOUSTON, SENIOR PASTOR, HILLSONG
CHURCH; AUTHOR OF *LIVE, LOVE, LEAD*

"Rich Wilkerson, Jr., could have been the king of sand castles—smart, talented, way too good looking for his own good! He chose instead to give his life for the One True Kingdom and to call the world to the One True King. *Sandcastle Kings* frees us from the illusion of all the kingdoms that cannot stand to become citizens of the only kingdom where all are free!"

—ERWIN RAPHAEL MCMANUS, FOUNDER OF
MOSAIC; AUTHOR OF *THE ARTISAN SOUL*

"Rich is a gifted communicator, and in *Sandcastle Kings* he compellingly puts forth the case for examining the foundations of our lives, the unsexy but vital underpinnings that he as a pastor is down in the dirt helping people repair each day."

—BROOKE FRASER, SONGWRITER
AND RECORDING ARTIST

"Rich Wilkerson makes religion cool. Especially for the millennial generation that is so busy living in a fast-paced, tech-driven world that sometimes they forget to look up from their smartphones and be inspired. And that's exactly what Rich does, he inspires us to always make time for faith, no matter how busy we are, and he does it in the most relatable, entertaining way. It's like having a best friend who can guide you through struggles, heartache, and life's biggest worries. He constantly amazes me with his love of all people and his genuine desire to help us all. He is the real deal."

—GUILIANA RANCIC, HOST OF *E! NEWS*,
FASHION POLICE; AND AUTHOR OF THE *NEW YORK
TIMES* BESTSELLER *GOING OFF SCRIPT*

"*Sandcastle Kings* will take you on a tour of life. The final destination may surprise you but will not disappoint. My friend Rich delivers an instant classic!"

—CHRIS DURSO

"This is not a book, it's a call to arms. Rich has clearly and passionately laid out a battle plan that will keep your life from becoming an empire of dirt and a story of what could have been. No matter what mistakes are behind you, *Sandcastle Kings* will help you build the kind of life you will want ten years from now and ten thousand years after that."

—LEVI LUSKO, PASTOR, FRESH LIFE CHURCH; AND
AUTHOR OF *THROUGH THE EYES OF A LION*

"Growing up with Rich, I knew he would impact people, but I underestimated by how much. I witnessed him writing some of this book on a vacation when he sat down and couldn't type all his thoughts out fast enough. I knew he was on to something and, after reading *Sandcastle Kings*, he delivered. I'm glad he gave up some of that trip to remind us about the importance of life's foundations. I'm forever changed."

—JASON KENNEDY, *E! NEWS* COHOST

"It doesn't take long to notice that Rich's life stands on a solid foundation that is much bigger than himself. The genuine passion that so evidently radiates through his teaching, his love for people, and his heart for life is evidence of this. *Sandcastle Kings* paints a profound picture of the unshakable story the Lord has built on His foundation for you and shakes the desire to build worth on a personal empire that will never fulfill."

—LAUREN SCRUGGS, FOUNDER OF *LOLOMAGAZINE* AND
THE LAUREN SCRUGGS KENNEDY FOUNDATION, AUTHOR
OF *STILL LOLO* AND *YOUR BEAUTIFUL HEART*

"I can't think of anyone more qualified to write on the subject of a spiritually bankrupt society. Rich Wilkerson, Jr., has dedicated his entire life to serving people in need of help. These aren't just observations on culture. This is a book written by a man who has successfully guided a countless number of people to the answer for all of life's problems: Jesus."

—CHAD VEACH, LEAD PASTOR OF ZOE CHURCH, LOS ANGELES,
CALIFORNIA; AND AUTHOR OF *UNREASONABLE HOPE*

"'[O]ne of the most 'in touch' leaders of our time . . . in touch with our generation and in touch with our God . . . a leader we can easily follow into modern revival."

—JERRY LORENZO MANUEL, FRIEND

SANDCASTLE KINGS

SANDCASTLE KINGS

Meeting Jesus in a Spiritually Bankrupt World

RICH WILKERSON, JR.

NELSON
BOOKS

An Imprint of Thomas Nelson

Published in Nashville, Tennessee, by Nelson Books, an imprint of Thomas Nelson. Nelson Books and Thomas Nelson are registered trademarks of HarperCollins Christian Publishing, Inc.

Unless otherwise noted, Scripture quotations are taken from the Holy Bible, New International Reader's Version®, NIrV®. Copyright © 1995, 1996, 1998, 2014 by Biblica, Inc.® Used by permission of Zondervan. All rights reserved worldwide. www.zondervan.com. The "NIrV" and "New International Reader's Version" are trademarks registered in the United States Patent and Trademark Office by Biblica, Inc.®

Scripture quotations marked NLT are taken from the Holy Bible, New Living Translation. © 1996, 2004, 2007, 2013 by Tyndale House Foundation. Used by permission of Tyndale House Publishers, Inc., Carol Stream, Illinois 60188. All rights reserved.

Scripture quotations marked PHILLIPS are taken from J. B. Phillips, "The New Testament in Modern English," 1962 edition by HarperCollins.

Scripture quotations marked ESV are taken from the ESV® Bible (The Holy Bible, English Standard Version®). Copyright © 2001 by Crossway, a publishing ministry of Good News Publishers. Used by permission. All rights reserved.

Scripture quotations marked THE MESSAGE are taken from The Message. Copyright © by Eugene H. Peterson 1993, 1994, 1995, 1996, 2000, 2001, 2002. Used by permission of Tyndale House Publishers, Inc.

Thomas Nelson, Inc., titles may be purchased in bulk for educational, business, fund-raising, or sales promotional use. For information, please e-mail SpecialMarkets@ThomasNelson.com.

Library of Congress Control Number: 2015943726
ISBN: 9780718032685

Printed in the United States of America

15 16 17 18 19 RRD 6 5 4 3 2 1

To my darling DawnCheré. Words will never do justice for the love I have for you. Thank you for coming on the journey. The best is yet to come.

CONTENTS

Contents

FOREWORD

IT HAS BEEN SAID THAT SOME THINGS ARE NOT WHAT they appear to be! And for the most part, that's true. Airports are less "hubs of travel" than they are "places to wait around for hours on end while you question the meaning of life." Krispy Kreme doughnuts *seem* like heaven, but in reality a steady diet of them will wreak havoc on you. Appearances can be deceiving! This is nowhere more true than in what we think will bring us fulfillment. We think that if we have more things, more success, more opportunity, more followers, more *money*, our shaky lives would find some balance, peace, and solidity. The problem is that our world is full of people who have achieved a "life of more," who have built empires and businesses and relationships on the idea of "more"—who are literally dying in pursuit of that idea of more—only to find out "more" is not what it appears. Worse yet, this pursuit just leaves them *more empty* than before. The diabolical reality is that sometimes we are the last to realize that a pursuit of more is a con, and by then it can seem too late. Blood, sweat, and tears litter the beaches of our society as the endless search for solid ground continues for many.

But there is a better way: an encounter with Jesus. And in this new book Rich Wilkerson, Jr., presents Jesus exactly as He is: the answer to *everything*. We can surrender our entire lives at the cross and rest in the peace of knowing that no matter what happens to "the things" of this world that undoubtedly will come and go, Jesus remains the same! Faithful and true. It may not appear obvious to most people that a carpenter from a small town, with no "earthly accolades" to his name and who walked the earth for only three decades, would hold all the keys to this life and eternity. But I believe it's true! And my prayer is that this important book will sound some alarms in the lives of many: those who have already seen the storms of this life shake them beyond belief and have had no protection as well as those who have yet to decide whether the search for "more" truly ends with Jesus. I pray the gospel truth shines through for them! I thank God for Rich Wilkerson, Jr., who is graced to enter the world of the "sandcastle kings" and lead many towards the real King and His unshakeable kingdom. This book is a blessing!

Carl Lentz
Hillsong NYC

INTRODUCTION

When I was fourteen, my parents packed up the Wilkerson family Suburban and moved my brothers and me from Tacoma, Washington, our beloved hometown, to Miami, Florida, a place as foreign to us as Mars. West Coast to East Coast. Cold to hot. Rain to sun. English to everything but English. 2,729 miles. It might as well have been two million. Everything was foreign. Everything, that is, except the beach. Even in dreary, rainy Tacoma, the Wilkerson clan shared beautiful days together at the local beaches. And Miami has one of the best beaches in the world. I loved everything about it. The waves, the sand, the sounds. But I especially loved building sandcastles.

Remember sandcastles? Remember how great it felt to dig your hands into that cool sand and fill your bucket with just the right type of sand—wet enough that it would stick together, but not so wet that you couldn't shape it? Remember packing the walls and bridges into place and filling the moat with enough sea water to drown any enemy foolish enough to attack your castle? My brothers and I spent hours on our sandcastles. One shovel-full at a time, we sculpted beautiful and imposing white-sand structures, painstakingly smoothing the edges and carving out windows and doors. We dug rivers and ponds, built towers and bridges, and carefully placed seashells all over (because, you know, that's what the princess would have wanted). We created the castles; we were the kings.

Eventually, our shoulders pink from too much sun, we would put on the finishing touches—a twig here, a little seaweed there—and admire what we had built. We then played on the beach for the rest of the day, glorying in our castle each time we walked past it. Except for the occasional errantly thrown football or clumsily placed foot, our sandcastles lasted all day, impervious to the ocean breezes and the sun's rays mercilessly shining down.

But then near the end of the day, when the sun began to set and the tide began to rise, we would remember what all sandcastle builders know and wish wasn't true. The ocean was going to destroy our sandcastle. It wouldn't be there in the morning. We would head home knowing that we would never see that castle again. The next day, as surely as the sun rises in the east, our castle would be gone. There would not be a trace of it—just flat, sandy beach as far as our eyes could see—as if we had never been there, as if all our hard work had never taken place. For all of our efforts, we were left only with the stinging sunburn earned the day before.

Here's something I've learned from reading the Bible: Children aren't the only ones building from sand and becoming sandcastle kings. Jesus explained it like this in Matthew's gospel:

> Everyone who hears these words of mine and puts them into practice is like a wise man who built his house on the rock. The rain came down, the streams rose, and the winds blew and beat against that house; yet it did not fall, because it had its foundation on the rock. But everyone who hears these words of mine and does not put them into practice is like a foolish man who built his house on sand. The rain came down, the streams rose, and the winds blew and beat against that house, and it fell with a great crash.
>
> MATTHEW 7:24–27

Jesus' point was straightforward. A house built on a solid foundation is strong and resilient; a house built on sand is weak and dangerous. When the storms come (storms always come sooner or later), the strong house will stand and the weak house will fall. This is common sense, right?

Unfortunately, when it comes to the way we build our lives, far too often we build on sand instead of on solid rock. For some people, their lives are based on money. For others, it's a relationship, or physical health, or fame, or knowledge, or even family. There may be as many faulty ways to build a life as there are grains of sand on the beach.

The problem is not that any of these things are bad. Most are good things, in and of themselves. That's why we can be so tempted to build our lives on them. Who doesn't want to do well at work, to have a strong marriage, to be healthy and educated and have great kids? These things are good. We should want them.

The problem comes when we make any of these *good* things our *foundational* thing. When we buy into the idea that some thing is the only thing that can make us happy and fulfilled, that thing takes priority in our lives. We chase it with all our strength.

When our foundation is money, we don't just work hard and do our best at our jobs. We work nights and weekends. We miss birthdays and recitals. We neglect family and friends. We never consider the personal price we're paying for success. We never think about what we might lose.

When our foundation is relationships, we don't just love people. We find our identity and worth in their love for us. We allow them to dictate who we are. We change the way we dress, the way we talk, the things we like to do, and even our morals, all in an attempt to get them to like us. We never stop to consider that the "us" we're trying to get them to like isn't really "us" at all. They are imposters, characters we're playing. We don't realize that if we wear the mask for too long, we might never be able to take it off.

When our foundation is physical health, we don't just exercise to feel better or to ward off disease. We exercise to look better than the person exercising beside us, so that our washboard abs or toned arms and legs are the envy of everyone at the beach. We exercise so that when we look in the mirror, we will like what we see on the outside without having to worry about who we are on the inside.

The goals and methods vary, but the outcome doesn't.

When we make a good thing a foundational thing, we set up ourselves for frustration, sorrow, and despair. However pretty the sandcastle looks, however strong you make its walls, however deep the moat, however high the towers, the waves will eventually knock it down, and the sandcastle kingdom will be washed away.

Scan the headlines of your favorite news website and you'll see this truth illustrated in the lives of the rich and famous. How many young pop stars had a meteoric rise, phenomenal success almost overnight, followed by erratic behavior, drug abuse, an unsuccessful stint in rehab, and then virtual anonymity? How many celebrity marriages ended in divorce before the honeymoon was over? How many business tycoons scraped and scammed their way to the top only to see their marriages unravel, their children grow up to hate them, and their companies embroiled in a corporate scandal? Sandcastle lives are everywhere. We read about them every day.

But it's not just in Hollywood or on Wall Street, is it? We all know people in our own circles who have similar stories. The workaholic neighbor whose twenty-year marriage is teetering on the verge of collapse. The alcoholic cousin who can't hold a job. The twice-divorced friend who keeps inviting you to meet her new boyfriend, enthusiastically insisting that "he's the one." The triathlete brother just diagnosed with terminal cancer.

Maybe you have lived such a story. Maybe you're living one right now. Storms come. Tides rise. The question is what will happen when the water crashes into your castle. Is it made of solid rock or shifting sand? The strong house will stand. The weak house will fall.

This book is about several people in the Bible whose houses, in whole or in part, were built on sand. The rain came, the river rose, the wind blew, and their houses crashed down around them. The lives were in turmoil. Their loved ones were sick or had died. They were outcasts in their communities. They lost hope. They were depleted, destitute, ruined. In a word, they were "bankrupt." You know the feeling, right? Many of us do. And we can usually feel the signs of it.

Although we don't like to admit it or think about it for too long, there's probably a longing deep inside that makes us anxious, uneasy, discontent. It makes us wish for something else, some other place, some other person, or job, or identity. We have little or no peace or rest. We yearn for more, or less, or just something different. We run frantically from one pleasure to the next, hoping desperately to find some sort of lasting contentment, eventually concluding that we "can't get no satisfaction."

Here's where we can learn from the experiences of the biblical people you will meet in this book. In the midst of their bankruptcies, at just the right time, they crossed paths with Jesus. Each person's story is different, but in each case, as the storm raged and the water rose, Jesus rushed into the collapsing castle, rescued the person, and put him or her on solid ground. It's heroic. It's beautiful.

These amazing stories are found in Luke chapter 7. "Chapter 7," you may know, is the name of one of the most common types of bankruptcy in the United States. Every year, nearly a million people file for Chapter 7 bankruptcy. When a person files under Chapter 7, the goal is to eliminate as many debts as possible. The process usually requires the debtor to sell the majority of his assets, and in many cases all of his debts are satisfied or dismissed and the debtor walks away with a fresh financial start. Creditors hate Chapter 7. Most of them don't get repaid. Instead, after verifying that the debtor is unable to repay his debts, the judge orders the debts to be dismissed, and the creditors' claims become unenforceable.

Luke chapter 7 carries stories that look similar to a Chapter 7 bankruptcy proceeding. The people are ruined, unable to meet the demands of their circumstances, unable to pay their debts—especially their biggest debt of all: their debt to God. Then Jesus enters their lives and they experience mercy and grace. Their debts are forgiven. They get a fresh start. Jesus restores the hope they feared was lost. Near the end of Luke 7, Jesus teaches his disciples through the following story:

> "Two people owed money to a certain moneylender. One owed him five hundred denarii, and the other fifty. Neither of them had the money to pay him back, so he forgave the debts of both. Now which of them will love him more?"
>
> Simon replied, "I suppose the one who had the bigger debt forgiven."
>
> "You have judged correctly," Jesus said.
>
> LUKE 7:41–43

God has forgiven the substantial debts in my life. I want you to experience the same freedom and peace that comes when Jesus dismisses your debts and gives you a fresh start. Wherever you are in your life—whether you have just arrived on the beach or the tide is now drowning the castle you have been building for years—I hope that this book helps you find solid ground. As we examine the stories in Luke 7, I want you to come to know that God, through Jesus, desires to rescue you from spiritual bankruptcy by forgiving the greatest debt you owe. Jesus wants you to stop building sandcastles and pretending that you are the king. He is the king, and he wants to help you build your life on the only foundation strong enough to withstand the storms of this life: himself.

Part One

THE BOSS

When Jesus had finished saying all this to the people who
were listening, he entered Capernaum. There a centurion's
servant, whom his master valued highly, was sick and about to
die. The centurion heard of Jesus and sent some elders of the
Jews to him, asking him to come and heal his servant. When
they came to Jesus, they pleaded earnestly with him, "This
man deserves to have you do this, because he loves our nation
and has built our synagogue." So Jesus went with them.
He was not far from the house when the centurion sent friends to
say to him: "Lord, don't trouble yourself, for I do not deserve to
have you come under my roof. That is why I did not even consider
myself worthy to come to you. But say the word, and my servant
will be healed. For I myself am a man under authority, with soldiers
under me. I tell this one, 'Go,' and he goes; and that one, 'Come,'
and he comes. I say to my servant, 'Do this,' and he does it."
When Jesus heard this, he was amazed at him, and turning to
the crowd following him, he said, "I tell you, I have not found
such great faith even in Israel." Then the men who had been
sent returned to the house and found the servant well.

Luke 7:1–10

Chapter One

CHECKLIST CHILDREN

When Jesus had finished saying all this to the people who were listening, he entered Capernaum. There a centurion's servant, whom his master valued highly, was sick and about to die. The centurion heard of Jesus and sent some elders of the Jews to him, asking him to come and heal his servant. When they came to Jesus, they pleaded earnestly with him, "This man deserves to have you do this, because he loves our nation and has built our synagogue." So Jesus went with them.

LUKE 7:1–6

GARAGE DUTY

My dad traveled regularly away from home when I was a kid. Most weeks he would fly out on Saturday morning and return the following Thursday. He was gone a lot, but that didn't stop him from being heavily involved in our day-to-day lives. He talked to us all the time, even when he was on the road, and he always made sure we knew that he was counting on my brothers and me to help Mom around the house. Before he left town each week he would make a detailed list of chore assignments for us. On one particular Saturday, my job was the garage.

I hated cleaning our garage. I mean, it was a garage! Why did it need to be cleaned? We kept garbage in there, for crying out loud! Now before you judge me for whining, you need to know that cleaning the Wilkerson family garage meant more than sweeping the floor and taking out the garbage cans. Cleaning that garage meant using geometry, or trigonometry, or one of those other "-ometrys" that you think you will never actually use in real life. My dad used colored tape to designate certain parts of the garage for certain items. The bikes had to go in the green zone and the tools in the red zone. In the yellow zone went the mower and other yard tools. The garbage cans had to go in the blue zone. Like a puzzle, everything had its place, and you had to place everything just right for it all to fit.

But on that Saturday, my friends and I planned to go to a movie premier early in the afternoon. I had been looking forward to it all week. Unfortunately, in the Wilkerson house if you didn't do your chores, you weren't allowed to go out with your friends. When I woke up late on that Saturday morning, I realized there was no way I could clean the garage and make it to the theater on time. So I had a choice. Clean the garage and miss the movie or go to the movie and ignore the garage. I consulted the little angel and devil that sit on my shoulders.

You can guess who I listened to. About fifteen minutes later, I was dressed and on my way to the movie. I met my friends, bought my popcorn, and sat down inside the theater. As soon as the lights went down, the reality of what I had just done sunk in. A sick feeling arose in the pit of my stomach. I don't remember what the movie was about. It didn't matter. I spent the whole time worrying about what Mom and Fad would do to me when they found out I had gone to the movies without finishing my chores. So to me it was a scary movie.

That night, when Dad called, Mom told him what I had done and then put me on the phone. "Richie," Dad said, "it's a good thing you saw that movie today because you're not going to be seeing one for a very long time! You're grounded until we're tired of having you around the house. And you've earned yourself garage duty for the next month."

The punishment fit the crime.

CHECKLIST CHILDREN

From the time we are very young, our parents reward us for doing what we are supposed to do and punish us for doing things we aren't supposed to do. If we do our chores, we get an allowance. If we don't clean the garage, we don't get to go to the movies. So very early on we learn what it means to "deserve." If we do good things we learn that we "deserve" good things. If we do bad things we learn that we "deserve" bad consequences. This concept is often called "justice," although our parents usually described it as "what's right" or "what's fair."

Understanding justice is an important part of a child's development, and we depend on the role of justice throughout our adult lives. Justice is one of the founding concepts of American society. We punish people for doing bad things, such as committing crimes, and we reward people for doing good things, such as when someone gets a raise for doing exceptionally good work.

Justice is important to us, and we have our own ideas about what it entails. So it's no surprise that when we think about God—ultimate arbiter and source of justice—we expect him to act according to what we think is just. When we do good things, like pray and attend church and walk a little old lady across the street, we expect God to bless us. When someone steals or spreads lies or kicks puppies, we expect God to punish that person. We think God has a checklist and is keeping score. If we have more checkmarks on the "good things" list than on the "bad things" list, God will reward us. If we have more "bad things," God will punish us. Behind this is the idea that we get what we deserve in life. We even have a mystical-sounding name for it: karma. So we have sayings such as: "What goes around comes around." We believe that good things happen to good people and bad things happen to bad people.

That's why it's so hard for us to understand why bad things happen to good people. When dad loses his job, or a favorite grandparent gets cancer, or a criminal escapes punishment, we feel that God isn't doing his part. Did he forget about his checklist? Did all those good things Grandma did not matter to God? We don't understand, so we're resigned to the idea that life (and God) just isn't fair. Well, sometimes life isn't fair, but sometimes it is fairer than we realize. When it comes to God, our concept of justice—the idea that we get what we deserve—is both more right and more wrong that we could ever imagine. More on that later. For now, let's talk about Roman soldiers.

THE CENTURION

WHEN JESUS HAD FINISHED SAYING ALL THIS TO the people who were listening, he entered Capernaum. There a centurion's servant, whom his master valued highly, was sick and about to die. The centurion heard of Jesus and sent some elders of the Jews to him, asking him to come and heal his servant.

LUKE 7:1–3

In the first few verses of Luke 7, Jesus was in a city called Capernaum, and by this point in his life he was fairly well known. He had been travelling through towns of the region, teaching about God and healing people. In the verses just before Luke 7, Jesus preached the Sermon on the Mount, saying, "Blessed are you who are poor," and "Love your enemies," and "Do not judge," and many other remarkable things.

Luke tells us that a large crowd followed Jesus. Some were eager to hear him speak. Others sought healing. Some simply wanted to see what all the fuss was about. Others wanted to be entertained, to see a miracle or two and call it a night. Whatever their motivations, people traveled from all over the country to see and hear Jesus. When Jesus came to town, it was a big deal. He was a celebrity, but without the money and sense of entitlement.

When Jesus gets to Capernaum, it does not take long for word to get out that he is there. Only two verses into Luke 7, we learn that Jesus is already the talk of the town. The news even makes its way to a certain Roman centurion.

Now, in case you slept through your ancient history class, let me tell you about Roman centurions. These dudes were hardcore. They were members of the Roman army, which at that time was the most fearsome and powerful military force the world had ever seen. Centurions commanded around one hundred soldiers. They were chosen to command based on their military experience, their skill with the various weapons, and the recommendations of other officers. Centurions were responsible for training and disciplining the soldiers within their "century," and they were paid well. They were intelligent, skilled, hardened, temperate, and extremely strict. Think of Maximus from the movie *Gladiator*. (I know, I know. Maximus was a general. But you get the idea.) These guys were not to be trifled with.

So in Luke 7, we read that this centurion had a servant who was so sick that he was near death. We don't know much about the servant, but Luke explains that the servant was especially important to the centurion. Maybe he was highly skilled or especially good at overseeing the centurion's other servants. Maybe he had become close to the centurion in some way. Whatever the case, the servant was important enough for the centurion to try to find him a cure. But nothing so far had worked. For all his power and wealth, the centurion had not been able to see his servant healed. When he heard about Jesus, the famous Jewish healer, the centurion decided to give him a shot.

In Luke 7, the centurion contacted the Jewish elders of Capernaum and asked them to speak to Jesus on his behalf. The centurion, familiar with authority and chain of command, may have believed that it would have been improper for him to go to Jesus directly, bypassing the Jewish elders who were in charge of the Jewish religious life of the city. So it may have been that, in an attempt to approach Jesus in the "proper" way, the centurion requested that the elders go to Jesus and ask him to heal his dying servant.

PLEASE, PLEASE, WITH A CHERRY ON TOP!

WHEN THEY CAME TO JESUS, THEY PLEADED EAR-nestly with him, "This man deserves to have you do this, because he loves our nation and has built our synagogue."

LUKE 7:4–5

The Jewish elders, however, did more than just take a polite request to Jesus. They "pleaded earnestly" with Jesus, assuring Jesus that the centurion was worthy of his help. They pointed to all the checkmarks the centurion had in the "good things" column. He loved Israel. He treated the Jews well. He had built them a synagogue to worship in.

There is an interesting dynamic at play here. At this point in history, the Roman Empire ruled the land of Israel, and the Roman army was a conquering force, a mortal enemy of the people of Israel. The centurion, as the authority in charge of the Roman soldiers in Capernaum, was one of the most powerful men in the city. He represented Rome, the largest and most powerful empire in the world. Capernaum was almost completely at his mercy. He had the power and authority to make life miserable for the locals, to impose the might of Rome with merciless brutality. But apparently he do not do that. Luke tells us that the elders were fond of the centurion, who loved the people and even built them a place of worship.

The elders spoke highly of the centurion, but his kindness may not have been altruistic. It was common for Roman officials to use measures other than force to keep a conquered people quiet. Uprisings and rebellions were destructive and expensive. If an official could appease the local population by relaxing a few laws or constructing a new building, the ensuing peace was worth the price.

Whether the centurion was a nice guy or not, the elders convinced Jesus to help his dying servant. They went straight to the checklist and pointed out all the "good things" the centurion had done for the Jews. But here's something the Bible tells us about God: He judges people based on what is in their hearts, not on the way things appear on the outside. In 1 Samuel 16:7, we read: "The LORD does not look at the things people look at. People look at the outward appearance, but the LORD looks at the heart." The elders tried to convince Jesus that the centurion had earned Jesus' help. They pointed out all the ways the centurion had helped the Jewish people in Capernaum.

The help was real and the elders' appreciation probably was real, but here's another truth the Bible teaches: when we do the right thing for the wrong reason, we don't earn any points with God. God judges our hearts and knows the true motivations for our actions. Ecclesiastes 7:20 puts it this way: "There is no one on earth who is righteous, no one who does what is right and never sins." Unfortunately, even our best deeds are tainted by the sin in our hearts. Isaiah 64:6 says, "All our righteous acts are like filthy rags." Without God giving us the power to choose good, it is impossible for us to do anything that is truly good. Our "good" deeds are worth as much to God as dirty, stinking rags.

Earlier I said that when it comes to God, our concept of justice—that we get what we deserve—is more right and more wrong than we ever could have imagined. It is right in the sense that God is just. "The LORD loves righteousness and justice" (Psalm 33:5); therefore, ultimately, "the wicked will not go unpunished" (Proverbs 11:21). But we go wrong in two ways. First, we are inconsistent in our desire for God to administer justice. If someone wrongs me, I want God to punish that person. Immediately. But when I'm in the wrong, I'm not so insistent that God punish the wrongdoer. And if I do something I think of as a good thing, I want God to reward me and to do it right now. If he doesn't, I get impatient and start to wonder whether he is just. Second, we give ourselves a lot more credit than we should. We don't think of our righteous acts as filthy rags, do we? We think of them as being pretty special, and we expect to get a little credit, a little pat on the back. The last thing we think is that our good deed was worthless.

Jesus knew all of this. So when the Jewish elders tried to convince him that the centurion was a good man, that he deserved Jesus' help, Jesus knew better. He knew the centurion was not a good man, not in the way God defines "good"—because no one is. The centurion wasn't righteous, because no man is righteous. Maybe the centurion only did those nice things because they lined up with his own selfish interests. Maybe not. Either way, even the centurion's best deeds were like filthy rags to God. The centurion didn't have enough good checkmarks on his list. In fact, he didn't have *any* good checkmarks on his list. Apart from God, none of us have any good checkmarks: "For all have sinned and fall short of the glory of God" (Romans 3:23). So the centurion didn't deserve Jesus' help. He never could have deserved it. Despite his power, his wealth, his connections, and all the good things he had done for the people of Capernaum, the centurion was morally and spiritually bankrupt, just like the rest of us are without God's help. It should surprise us, then, what Jesus did next.

AMAZING GRACE

JESUS WENT WITH THEM.

LUKE 7:6

13

Wait a minute! What? Jesus knew that the centurion did not deserve his help, that the centurion's checklist read something like: "Good deeds: 0. Bad deeds: Many." He knew that even the best things the centurion ever did were as valuable as filthy rags to God. He knew that he did not owe the centurion anything. Yet, "Jesus went with them."

What gives? Didn't Jesus understand justice? Didn't he know that people are supposed to get what they deserve? Had he never heard of karma?

Well, Jesus probably never used the word *karma*, but he knew all about justice. He invented it. In John 1:3, we read that through Jesus "all things were made; without him nothing was made that has been made." All things. Including justice. Jesus knew what the centurion deserved and didn't deserve, but Jesus also knew that there was something far more important than administering justice in that moment. Jesus knew the two greatest commandments: "Love the Lord your God with all your heart and with all your soul and with all your mind and with all your strength," and, "Love your neighbor as yourself" (Mark 12:30–31).

Jesus could have denied the centurion's request. He did not owe the centurion his help. But in that moment Jesus recognized an opportunity to glorify God by loving his neighbor, the centurion, and to demonstrate to everyone in Capernaum what it looks like to truly "love your enemies" (Matthew 5:44). So Jesus went with the Jewish elders.

Chapter Two

WE'RE NOT WORTHY

So Jesus went with them.
He was not far from the house when the centurion sent
friends to say to him: "Lord, don't trouble yourself, for I do
not deserve to have you come under my roof. That is why
I did not even consider myself worthy to come to you."

Luke 7:6–7

Airport Lines

Been to an airport lately? It's insane. Everyone is in a gigantic hurry, from the second you pull into the parking lot to the blessed moment when you finally take your seat on the plane. Taxicab drivers, parking-lot attendants, the people at the ticket counter, the agents at the security checkpoints, the pilots . . . everyone seems to be in full-scale panic, and many may be in a bad mood. It's like they're all auditioning to be that family from *Home Alone*—the McCallisters, right? I would have made an amazing Kevin. But I digress.

Chaos is the norm at the airport. People are sleep-deprived, late, overworked, and under-caffeinated. They're toting bags that weigh three times their body weight. It's stressful, to say the least. At the heart of the insanity is the most stress-inducing factor of all: the lines. The lines at the airport never seem to end. You have to wait in line to get into the parking lot. You wait in line to check in. You wait in line at security. You wait in line at the bathroom, in the food court, to get on the plane, to get off the plane, at baggage claim, at the taxi stand—everywhere! And because there are so many lines, people tend to get behind schedule, which leads to stress, which leads to impatience, which leads to flared tempers, which leads to arguing, which leads to a security officer inviting you to spend some time behind the glass wall, where he will politely question you regarding your country of origin and your intended destination.

Now, I can deal with most of the stress: the lines, the crying baby, the clumsy packrat, and pretty much everything else, except for the line-cutter. Remember that guy? You went to elementary school with him. We all did. He was the one who always came out of nowhere and jumped in front of everybody else, whether it was his day to be "line leader" or not. Yeah, that guy. He's still around and still up to his old shenanigans. Don't believe me? Go to the airport. After you have waited patiently in the parking lot line, the elevator line, and the longer-than-the-equator check-in line, this guy will come out of nowhere and stroll right up to the counter ahead of you. He wasn't even in line. He waltzed into the airport like he owned the place, walked right past the fifteen or so people in line (including you), strutted up to the counter, and started talking to the ticket lady as if you weren't even standing there. Now, I'm a patient guy—well, I'm working on it—but a line-cutter can cause this pastor to experience some righteous anger!

Kidding aside, think about how you feel when someone cuts in front of you. You might say something, or you might not, but I'm guessing it makes you angry. Why? *Because it's not fair.* You waited patiently in line, as you were supposed to, and that person didn't. He cheated. If you let him get away with it, he will get what he doesn't deserve. What he deserves is to be sent to the end of the line, or worse. If this guy didn't wake up early enough (like you did), or get packed soon enough (like you did), or arrive on time (like you did), then he doesn't deserve to be at the front of the line (where you are). He didn't earn that spot at the front. You did. And so he can just go take his place at the rear, thank you very much, and maybe next time he will get there a little sooner. It's only *fair*.

Now, fairness and justice are good things. God loves both. In fact, God is more just than we might want him to be. Ultimately, he will judge all of our good and bad deeds. But if we think of God *only* as just, then our understanding of God is seriously lacking.

JUST DESSERTS

Around three thousand years ago a man named Moses climbed to the top of a mountain, where God gave him the laws that God's people were to follow. We call these the Ten Commandments. You might remember a few of them. Do not murder. Do not steal. Do not lie.

You can find all ten in Exodus 20:1–17. Throughout the Old Testament, God gave his people many more laws, and the priests and teachers devised rules and guidelines to help the people follow all the laws.

When God first gave Moses the Ten Commandments, God wrote them on two stone tablets. You ever heard the phrase "written in stone"? This is where that came from. When we say something is "written in stone," we mean we can't change it, can't erase it, can't undo it. The Ten Commandments literally were written in stone. They are rigid and unchangeable. They represent the eternal, unchanging character of God. They tell us something about who God is and what God expects from us. God is holy and his standard is exceptionally high.

It is so high, in fact, that none of us will ever live up to it. Have you ever told a lie? Have you ever been envious of something someone has? Have you ever disrespected your parents? If so, then you have violated God's law, and the Bible tells us that violating one of the laws is the same as violating all of the laws. James 2:10 says, "For whoever keeps the whole law and yet stumbles at just one point is guilty of breaking all of it."

God's law can seem rigid and harsh. But it is also wonderful. It tells us that God is just, that he is good and loves goodness. Have you ever thought about that? What if God were not good? What if he did not love justice? He could have given us laws that told us to hate one another, to hurt one another, to lie, to cheat, to steal. But he did not do that. He gave us laws that tell us to do good to one another, to help one another, to not hurt one another.

Even worse, what if God never spoke at all? What if God just left us on our own to figure things out for ourselves? What on earth might we think up? Without God's law, we would have been left with raw, dog-eat-dog, survival-of-the-fittest competition. The powerful would prey on the weak, and there would be no hope of something better. But God did not leave us here on earth without any idea of who he is, and he gave us his law to help us understand him better. The Law tells us that God is good and that he wants us to be good too.

Unfortunately for us, when we look at God's law and then look at ourselves, it doesn't take long to realize how far we fall short of God's standard. We might do some good things, but we aren't perfect. In fact, we say "I'm not perfect" whenever we want to justify some wrong thing that we did. We are not holy, as God is holy. We are not even close.

In our effort to "make up" for our shortcomings, we try harder. We help more old ladies across the street. We volunteer at the soup kitchen for a few hours. We throw a little more money in the offering plate at church. We do whatever we think it takes to tip the scales back in our favor. But the Bible tells us that no matter how hard we try, we can never make up for our shortcomings. No matter how many old ladies make it across the street under our care, no matter how many homeless people we feed, no matter how much money we give away, once we break God's laws we can never un-break them.

God's law is a gift because it shows us something about who God is. But God's law is also a burden. We can never live up to God's perfect standard. We will always fall short. We will always need to do more. The Law makes demands; it does not give us rest.

Here's the good news: In addition to being just, God is infinitely merciful. He is so merciful that he sent his son to earth to help us. John 1:17 tells us that although God gave us the Law through Moses, he gave us "grace and truth" through Jesus. There is so much in that little phrase, "grace and truth." When Jesus came to earth it would have been entirely fair for him to have cracked us over the head for failing to follow God's laws. That would have been justice. And it would have made a good movie. The hero shows up to punish all the lawbreakers and make everything right. Everyone in the audience would have cheered. Unfortunately, everyone in the audience *is* the law-breaker. If Jesus had come to earth to punish all the wrongdoers, he would have had to punish everyone. That would have been fair, but it would not have been nice for us.

The great news is that God did not send Jesus to earth to punish everyone for breaking the Law. John 3:17 tells us, "God did not send his Son into the world to condemn the world, but to save the world through him." How amazing is that? God gives us his law, his standard—what we would have to do in order to be considered "good"—and every single one of us breaks the Law. We fall short. We are not "good" people. But instead of sending lightning bolts from heaven, God sent Jesus, "full of grace and truth," to save the world. Amazing! Jesus lets us in on how he is going to save the world in Matthew 5:17: "Do not think that I have come to abolish the Law or the Prophets; I have not come to abolish them but to fulfill them." Jesus came to save the world, not by destroying the Law that we could not fulfill, but by fulfilling the Law in a way that we never could.

In baseball, sometimes the manager uses a pinch hitter, whose job is to enter the game to bat in someone else's place. Usually the pinch hitter substitutes for a batter who isn't a good hitter. In this silly analogy we are the hitter who isn't very good. In fact, we strike out a lot. And the pitcher is perfect. Every pitch goes exactly where it's supposed to go. And the stadium is huge. The wall is so far away that even if we managed to hit a pitch, we could never hit a home run. About two thousand years ago, God sent Jesus into the game to bat in our place. And Jesus is a home run hitter. When he came to bat he belted the first pitch right out of the park.

I don't know about you, but this sounds like pretty great news to me. God knows that I could never meet his standard, his Law, so he sent Jesus to fulfill the Law on my behalf. And Jesus came "full of grace and truth," not more law. He gives me mercy when I deserve punishment, forgiveness rather than condemnation, freedom instead of bondage, and rest instead of work. This is good news. Great news! This is what the New Testament calls the "gospel," which means "good news."

When I was a kid, my brother and I got into many fights with each other. Every time we had a fight, I knew Mom or Dad would break it up and make us apologize to each other. My brother was always quick to say he was sorry. I hated that. And I almost never forgave him immediately. I always thought, *You're just saying what you need to say so you won't get in more trouble. You don't mean it. You aren't sorry.* So I wouldn't accept his apology right away. I would sulk and pout. I would act passive-aggressively, wanting my brother to hurt the way he hurt me. Deep down, I was thinking, *You don't deserve my forgiveness. You haven't earned it. I'm not going to forgive you until you feel my pain and understand how you have offended me. Only then will I think about forgiving you. You have to earn it. It's only fair.* If you have a brother or a sister, you understand where I was coming from.

But grace is anything but fair. Grace means getting something good without earning it. It's not fair. The Bible tells us that Jesus was "full of grace," not full of fairness. The fact is, when it comes to God, we really don't want what we deserve. We know we don't measure up to God's standard, which is perfection. Absolute perfection. In every way. Are you perfect?

I'm not. Far from it. But we don't like to talk about deserving God's punishment for our wrongdoings. Because of the gospel, however, God does not want to give us what we deserve. Jesus came so that we could experience the unmerited favor of God, so that we could have life and have it abundantly. What a gift!

And yet, time and time again I meet people who just won't let go of their checklists. They keep pointing to the "good things" they have done, trying to balance out the failings and mistakes. Often behind checklisting lies a refusal to believe that God could love people like them, that God could forgive them for the things they have done. So they keep trying to earn the forgiveness and love that only comes by grace. They get hung up on questions like, "Does God love me? Could I ever be valuable to him? Have I done enough to get his attention?" Their identity is all about *what they do* instead of *who God is*. They stay away from Jesus because they feel guilty for failing. But the forgiveness they so desire can never be found apart from Jesus.

JESUS WENT

Now back to the centurion. Jesus is on his way to the centurion's house when Luke tells us something remarkable:

> [Jesus] was not far from the house when the centurion sent friends to say to him: "Lord, don't trouble yourself, for I do not deserve to have you come under my roof. That is why I did not even consider myself worthy to come to you.
>
> LUKE 7:6–7

This is fascinating. Before Jesus reached the centurion's house, the centurion sent some friends to tell Jesus not to come. Just three verses earlier, the centurion had sent his friends to beg Jesus to come. What gives? I think the centurion was like some of us. He knew he needed Jesus' help, but he also knew he did not deserve Jesus' help.

The closer Jesus gets to us, the more we realize just how far we are from him, how far short we fall of his purity, wisdom, and holiness. When the centurion realized that Jesus was getting close, he panicked. He knew he was not worthy. By his own words we know he did not deserve to have Jesus come under his roof. "What if Jesus comes inside? What if he sees what a mess my house is? What if he sees what a mess my life is?" It breaks my heart to know that many people think this way. Jesus wants to come to their house, but when he gets close they panic and send him away.

We know we need his help, but we know we don't deserve it. And we're embarrassed because we have failed, because our lives are a mess, and because we know we are unable to clean up the mess. So we panic and turn Jesus away. Ironically and tragically, although we may refuse Jesus because we think we could never deserve him, we can never deserve him unless we accept him. Jesus knows we are like sick people in need of a doctor. He does not expect us to heal ourselves before we see the doctor. In Luke 5:31–32, Jesus says, "It is not the healthy who need a doctor, but the sick. I have not come to call the righteous, but sinners to repentance."

Isn't it silly? We know that we have made a mess of our lives, that we fall short of God's perfect standard. Yet, for some reason, we will not let Jesus get close. We want to clean things up before we let him in. We want to deserve his presence, but part of us knows we never could.

At the heart of this sort of thinking is pride. Among other things, pride means "an excessively high opinion of one's importance." This is about focusing on ourselves. When we are proud (and we are all proud), we are all about us. We might think well of ourselves or poorly of ourselves, but we don't stop thinking about ourselves. Our "self" is the problem, not the solution. Jesus is the solution. As long as I am focused on me, I will have a hard time seeing him.

Pride is one of those bad foundations. It is a house built on sand. We can dress it up, call it something nicer, like self-confidence, and even make it respectable, but when the waves start crashing into it, pride crumbles like the sandcastle it is. We can't depend on it because we can't depend on ourselves.

If I am honest with myself, I know that no one has let me down more than I have let down myself. No one has disappointed me more than myself. No one has broken more promises to me than I have broken to myself. For some reason, though, I have this tendency to keep trusting in myself. "Next time I'll do better," I think. And so I rebuild the sandcastle. We even encourage each other to do this. We say, "You can do it. Just believe in yourself." There's a place for that kind of advice, but when it comes to our relationship with God, we can't do it. But for some reason we keep trying.

One time in high school I put fifty cents in a vending machine and pushed the button for Cherry Coke, but nothing came out. I hit another button, and nothing came out. I put in another fifty cents and hit the button again. Nothing. I kicked the machine and muttered a few choice words. Once again, nothing came out. As I was about to lose it, a friend walked by and said, "Hey, man, don't you see the sign?" I looked at the side of the machine and saw a big yellow sign that read OUT OF ORDER.

I could have put my life savings into that machine and kicked it until my foot was black and blue and yelled until my voice was gone. None of that would have made any difference. The machine was out of order. Without Jesus, our lives are like that, out of order and incapable of giving us what we need, no matter how hard we try to make it work.

NOT GOOD ENOUGH

At this point, you might be tempted to respond in a couple of ways. First, you might disagree with me. "Rich," you might say, "you don't know what you're talking about. I've made it this far relying on myself. No one else is looking out for me, so I have to look out for myself." I understand where you're coming from, especially if you had parents who did not love and support you the way parents are supposed to. If you basically had to raise yourself, I commend you. I know how unbelievably hard that is to do. But please do not make the mistake of thinking that you have to rely on yourself to earn your way to God. You can't, and God doesn't want you to. He made the way, and the way is named Jesus.

Second, you might buy into what I'm saying. You agree that you cannot earn your way to God. You agree that you are your own worst enemy, that no one has disappointed you more than you have disappointed yourself. You know you are a sinner. You know you are a mess. You might even believe that you are worthless.

Dear friend, please believe me when I say that you are not worthless. You are loved. The almighty Creator God loves you so much that he sent his son to save you. Your deeds may be worthless, but you are not. If you believe in God, and if you believe that God is in control of the world, then you have to acknowledge that you are here by design. His design. In other words, God put you here on this earth on purpose. Your life is part of his plan, and he has a plan for your life.

Think about this. Just before you were conceived there was a gigantic race. The single cell that would eventually combine with another single cell to become you outraced 280 million other cells that were not you. 280 million! That's more than the population of Russia, Germany, and South Korea combined. Out of 280 million cells, you won the race. Think about how amazing this is. Your odds of winning were 1 in 280 million. To put that in perspective, your chances of winning the Powerball lottery are 1 in 175 million. So it is more likely that you will win the lottery than beat out all those other cells and come into existence. And yet, here you are! You won the race.

If you believe that God is in control of this world, that means that out of at least 280 million other options he chose to make you—you, with your pimples, frizzy hair, and nasal voice. You were "fearfully and wonderfully" made by God (Psalm 139:14). Do you know what else God says about you? Ephesians 2:10 indicates that in Jesus you are God's masterpiece. Now a masterpiece is an artist's best piece of work. God—the God who made the universe, the God who made the Big Dipper, the Pacific Ocean, the Grand Canyon, the gigantic sequoia tree, the delicate rose, and every amazing and beautiful creature walking and swimming and flying through this world—that God thinks of you as his masterpiece.

Look at it this way. The value of a thing is often based on what a buyer is willing to pay for it. When my wife and I moved to Miami in 2007, we needed a place to live, searched for the perfect place, and eventually found it. It was a beautiful modern-looking condo right in the heart of town. We gathered up our money, borrowed some more, and bought the unit. We loved that condo, and we paid a good chunk of money for it. Still, we believed we were getting a great deal. Then the financial crisis of 2008 happened, the real estate market plummeted, and we quickly found ourselves in the unfortunate situation that many Americans faced. Our condo was worth less than we paid for it. To us, it was still worth more than we had paid, but to the real estate market all that mattered was that no buyer was willing to pay what we had paid for it. Value was dictated by the buyer.

Now, the same is true of you and me. John 3:16 tells us: "God so loved the world that he gave his one and only Son, that whoever believes in him shall not perish but have eternal life." If you read the rest of the story, you see that God did not send Jesus to earth just to make friends with all of us. Jesus lived an amazing life, a perfect life, and then he was killed on a cross. None of this surprised God. Actually, it was God's plan.

He loved the world (including you) so much that he sent his son to save it, knowing all the while that Jesus would be tortured and killed. God believed you were worth it. So the next time you start thinking you are worthless, remember that your value is based on what God paid for you. God bought you with the blood of his son, Jesus Christ. Your value is not decided by what you do or do not do. It is based on what Jesus did. You are not worthless. You are priceless.

The best gift I ever got as a child was a crisp $100 bill from my grandpa. It was fresh from the bank, no wrinkles, no bent corners. I remember his telling me to save it. I think I kept it for about a week, until it burned a hole in my pocket and I spent the whole thing. Now, I don't care how old you are. Having an extra $100 to spend is exciting, whether the money is brand-new and wrinkle-free or crumpled and dirty. You can put it through the washing machine and it will still be worth $100. Its value is not based on its condition. It is based on what someone will give you for it, and a hundred dollars is a hundred dollars, no matter how wrinkled it is.

Maybe you have been through some rough stuff in your life. Maybe you are not proud of all the decisions you have made. I know I'm not. You know you haven't measured up to God's standard, but that does not mean you are not valuable to God. The fact is, despite your choices, despite your past, despite your wrinkles, your value in God's eyes has not changed. Like the centurion, you may not be worthy of God, but you are still priceless to him. And he alone gets to decide your worth.

Jesus has made himself available to you. You might not

feel worthy to come to him, but he is trying to get to you. He loves you and came to this earth to save you, to give you a future and a hope. Jesus went to the centurion because he loved him. It wasn't about the centurion. It was about Jesus. It's all about Jesus.

Chapter Three

HOW TO AMAZE JESUS

"But say the word, and my servant will be healed. For I myself am a man under authority, with soldiers under me. I tell this one, 'Go,' and he goes; and that one, 'Come,' and he comes. I say to my servant, 'Do this,' and he does it." When Jesus heard this, he was amazed at him, and turning to the crowd following him, he said, "I tell you, I have not found such great faith even in Israel." Then the men who had been sent returned to the house and found the servant well.

LUKE 7:7–10

DANCE PARTY

I grew up in a strong and strict Christian home. I'm a fourth-generation preacher. My dad, my grandfather, and my great-grandfather were preachers. I don't know what my great-great-grandfather was, but his son was a preacher, and that's pretty good, I guess.

When your grandfather and your dad are preachers, you find yourself in church a good bit. Actually, you find yourself in church all the time. All the time. Growing up, church was not just a part of my life. Church was my life. I was there every day of the week. Our weekly schedule looked something like this:

- SUNDAY: Morning service, Sunday
  school, night service
- MONDAY: A Taste of New Wine (the Christian
  "Alcoholics Anonymous")
- TUESDAY: Choir practice
- WEDNESDAY: Youth group
- THURSDAY: W.O.W. (Women of the Word)
  Bible study
- FRIDAY: Youth outreach night
- SATURDAY: Sidewalk Sunday school

Next time you complain about having to go to church a couple of times every week, just imagine little twelve-year-old Richie Wilkerson heading over to God's house every Monday night for the church version of AA: "Hi, everyone. I'm Richie, and I'm ... well ... I'm not an alcoholic but I sure do like grape juice. Pray for me."

Growing up in a preacher's house, we kids had all sorts of rules to obey. For example, we were not supposed to say certain words or watch certain movies. And, by golly, we were not supposed to dance, at least not in certain ways in certain places. Now if we were in church and the music was right and the service was rocking, we were encouraged to dance just like King David danced "unto the Lord." But outside the church house, dancing was forbidden, especially guy-girl dancing.

When my thirteenth birthday rolled around, however, I knew exactly what I wanted. It wasn't new shoes, or a new bike, or a new gaming system. I asked my parents to let me have a "boys and girls together" party, with dancing. You would have thought I had asked for a machine gun or a heroin party. They were adamantly opposed, but I'm a persuasive guy, and I can also be stubborn and super annoying. I begged and pleaded for so long that they eventually gave in, but with a few stipulations. The party would have to be at the old Wilkerson estate (my parents' house), and my family—parents, grandparents, aunts, uncles—would have to be there to chaperone. I reluctantly agreed.

When the night of the party finally rolled around, I was ready. My hair was gelled. My Nikes were spotless. My Tommy Hilfiger shirt was at least two sizes too big (give me a break; it was the '90s). I was turning thirteen and it was time to become a man. By dancing with a girl.

I told the DJ to play the most romantic song I could think of: "Awesome God" by Rich Mullins. Seriously. That's the one I chose. I mean really, is there any lyric that makes a girl swoon more than, "And the Lord wasn't jokin' when he kicked 'em out of Eden"? (You can't make this stuff up.)

So there I was, the preacher's kid, dancing (DANCING!) with a girl (WITH A GIRL!) in my house in front of my parents, grandparents, aunts, and uncles to "Awesome God." I was the epitome of cool and I knew it. (When you're thirteen, and your whole family is in the pastorate, and all you know is church, your idea of cool is a little skewed.)

You probably did not grow up going to church every day. And you probably did not dance your first slow dance to "Awesome God." But you absolutely have a perspective on life. We all do. Odds are, yours, like mine, was largely shaped by your childhood. Maybe you had two loving parents who had you in church all the time. Maybe you didn't. Maybe your parents divorced when you were little and you only got to see one of them on weekends and holidays, or less often. Maybe you never knew one of your parents. Maybe you never went to church. Maybe your childhood was better than I could even imagine. Maybe it was worse. Wherever you are coming from, you are coming from somewhere, and that somewhere shaped your perspective on life. Some people see life through a perspective of hurt. Some have a perspective of need. Others have a perspective of bitterness or cynicism or unhappiness.

People's perspectives are shaped by something in their

pasts, and whatever it is, good or bad, it tends to render them unable to see the world clearly, like putting on glasses with the wrong prescription. When our perspective is warped, we have a hard time seeing the truth.

Because of our sin we have a warped perspective when it comes to recognizing who is actually in charge in our lives. From the time we are very young, we believe that we are in control. We believe that we are the boss. When things go the way we want them, all is well. When things do not go our way, we throw a fit, stomp our feet, pout, or break things. (If you think toddlers are the only ones throwing fits, then you are not familiar with road rage, or verbal abuse, or sports fans.)

Our perspective of who is in control is warped. No matter how many times we are proven wrong, we keep thinking that we can control the world around us. In other words, we think we are God. As we have seen several times already, that is simply not the case, and part of what it means to know Jesus is simply recognizing that we are not God. Simple, right? It is simple, but for a lot of people it is not easy.

PERSPECTIVE

Imagine you have a pair of eyeglasses with blue lenses. If you look through those blue lenses at a banana or a school bus, they might be as yellow as Big Bird, but as long as you wear those glasses the banana and the school bus will appear to be green. The lens through which we see the world colors our perspective.

Everyone is wearing glasses of perspective, and the tint of

each person's lens is different. I don't see the world the same as you. I don't even see it the same as my wife. Sometimes my perspective is accurate. Many times it is not. When we see the world through an inaccurate lens, our view of reality is blurred. Our lens may lead us to believe that we are ultimately in control of our lives, that what we say goes. Our perspective can be so blurry that we see ourselves as God.

Over the years I have met many people. And because I speak for a living, I have had the opportunity to host a couple of TV shows where I talk with celebrities. Time and time again I have seen that the most successful people often are the most tormented. The people with the most stuff often experience the most sadness. You can be filthy rich and have all the toys that money can buy and yet have a soul that is utterly empty. In his song "All Falls Down," Kanye West said it like this:

It seems we livin' the American dream,
But the people highest up got the lowest self-esteem.

Often people with the greatest material success deal with the most spiritual and emotional pain. No amount of money or houses or stuff can fill the emptiness deep in a person's heart. No matter how hard you might try, you can never fill that void yourself.

Some people live their whole lives seduced by success. If they could just make a little more, if their net worth could be just a little higher, if they could just move into *that* neighborhood, or drive *that* car, or join *that* club everything would be okay. Then the uneasy feeling they wake up with every morning would finally go away. The anxiety every night would finally cease. So they climb that corporate ladder, or grind away building that business, and eventually they succeed. They get the raise. Their stock portfolio swells. They move into that house. They buy that car. And they play golf at that exclusive club. And yet they have no peace. The anxiety remains, and they don't understand why. They finally arrived at the place where they thought they would find contentment, but it's not there. The truth is, contentment is not found in a place. Contentment is found in a person: Jesus Christ.

In our story, the Roman centurion had a change of perspective. Many people around him believed that he was worthy of Jesus' help, but the centurion saw himself more clearly. So instead of using his own authority and reputation to force Jesus to help his servant, this powerful Roman commander confessed that he was empty, even hopeless, without Jesus. Once, the centurion probably thought—like most of us think—that he could solve his problems using his own power and intellect, but in a dire circumstance he confessed his need for Jesus' help. He could not change the situation. He did not have the power. He had great authority, but even his authority had a limit. So he went to Jesus, the only person with the power to give him peace in his pain.

You cannot come to Jesus until you stop going to yourself. Sometimes, all it takes is a change in perspective. We need to remove the blurry glasses that make us believe we are God. We need to see our lives in light of the truth that Jesus is Lord. Only in the truth will we find freedom from the ridiculously inaccurate perspectives we have and freedom from the bitterness, anxiety, and cynicism of those perspectives. Jesus is the truth. Only he can give you the peace you crave.

Jesus Was Amazed

Not too long ago my wife, DawnCheré, and I were invited to a birthday party for a family friend. This man is older and very accomplished, with all the trappings of material wealth— houses, cars, clothes, you name it. The guy has everything. As the date of the party approached, DawnCheré and I discussed what gift we would buy our friend. We dearly love this man, and we wanted our gift to express that. We ran through our options, frantically searching online and scouring the nearest shopping malls for that one special gift, the one he would cherish, the one he would open and be amazed by our thoughtfulness. We looked and looked, but to no avail. What do you give a man who has everything? We had no idea what we were looking for. If you don't know what you're looking for, you probably aren't going to find it. And we didn't.

Now, our friend is a special person, but what do you think it would take to impress the God of the universe? What could we possibly do or give or say that would make God say, "Wow!"?

In Luke 7:7–8, we find something remarkable. Remember the story so far: The Roman centurion has a very sick servant and the centurion wants Jesus to heal the servant. Jesus begins making his way to the centurion's house, but before Jesus gets there the centurion sends a messenger to tell Jesus not to come. Strange, isn't it? If the centurion wanted Jesus' help, why would he turn around and tell Jesus not to come? The centurion, through his messenger, tells Jesus,

> "I did not even consider myself worthy to come to you. But say the word, and my servant will be healed. For I myself am a man under authority, with soldiers under me. I tell this one, 'Go,' and he goes; and that one, 'Come,' and he comes. I say to my servant, 'Do this,' and he does it."
>
> LUKE 7:7–8

The centurion was familiar with authority. He commanded other men and he expected those men to respect his authority the same way he respected his superiors' authority. He knew that the Roman army owed its strength to the discipline of its soldiers, to their ability to respect and obey authority regardless of their personal preferences. When the centurion gave an order, it was followed.

The centurion understood that Jesus was in a position of authority. But Jesus' authority was different, and far greater, than the centurion's. The centurion had heard the stories about Jesus healing people of disease and making the lame to walk, the blind people see, and the deaf people hear. The centurion recognized what was going on: Jesus had authority over nature. Jesus did not have one hundred soldiers at his command. He had the entire creation at his command. In the same way that the centurion knew his orders would be obeyed, even from a distance, he recognized that Jesus could merely speak a word and creation would obey him.

Whether or not the centurion understood it at the time,

he was making a bold claim. The Jews in Jesus' day knew that only one person had ultimate authority over nature: God. Creation listens to God's words. In fact, God created the entire world just by speaking. By claiming that Jesus could control the natural world merely by speaking, the centurion associated Jesus with the all-powerful Creator God. At Jesus' word—just like at God's—creation would obey. The centurion recognized this and he trusted Jesus. In other words, the centurion had faith.

Luke tells us that when Jesus heard the centurion's message, Jesus was amazed. Did you catch that? Jesus—the second person in the holy Trinity, the God-man, the Word of Life, the one by whom and for whom all things were made—was amazed. Amazed! Amazed at what?

> When Jesus heard [the centurion speak] . . . he said, "I tell you, I have not found such great faith even in Israel."
>
> LUKE 7:9

Great faith. The centurion was an impressive guy, but it was not his power, status, or authority that amazed Jesus. It was not his morality or the good things he had done for the local Jewish community. It was his great faith that amazed Jesus.

When the centurion's servant got sick, the centurion did not invite Jesus in for a chat about healing. He did not ask for Jesus' credentials, or where Jesus had gone to medical school, or how he was able to heal people, or anything of that sort. Instead, he placed his faith in Jesus and confessed that all he needed was for Jesus to speak a word and his servant would be healed. And that is exactly what happened. And in the process, we find out that Jesus was amazed by the centurion's great faith.

There is only one other account in Scripture where Jesus is said to have been amazed. It is found in the sixth chapter of Mark.

> Jesus left there and went to his hometown, accompanied by his disciples. When the Sabbath came, he began to teach in the synagogue, and many who heard him were amazed.
>
> "Where did this man get these things?" they asked. "What's this wisdom that has been given him? What are these remarkable miracles he is performing? Isn't this the carpenter? Isn't this Mary's son and the brother of James, Joseph, Judas and Simon? Aren't his sisters here with us?" And they took offense at him.
>
> Jesus said to them, "A prophet is not without honor except in his own town, among his relatives and in his own home." He could not do any miracles there, except lay his hands on a few sick people and heal them. He was amazed at their lack of faith.
>
> MARK 6:1–6

This is an alarming story. Jesus is in his hometown, where you would think he will be welcomed with love and gladness. But Jesus isn't celebrated at all. He is barely tolerated. The people of the town are skeptical of his ministry. They criticize him. They mock his past and assume they know all there is to know about him. And Jesus was amazed at their lack of faith.

In the Scripture, two things amaze Jesus:

1. Great faith.
2. Lack of faith.

When Jesus looks at your life, what does he see? Great faith? Or no faith at all? Does your life amaze Jesus?

Great Faith

If great faith amazes Jesus, we probably ought to ask, "Just what is faith?" Simply put, faith means trusting without necessarily fully understanding. Understanding is a good thing. Knowledge is good. Wisdom is even better. But in Luke 7, it is not the centurion's knowledge or wisdom that amazed Jesus. It is his faith, his trust in Jesus, even though he doesn't completely understand. He believes that Jesus has some sort of power, and he believes that Jesus' power is based on some authority over creation, but the centurion likely cannot explain more than that. He simply trusts Jesus, a trust demonstrated by his insistence that a mere word from Jesus is enough to heal his servant. Jesus' word was enough for the centurion.

The Bible tells us in Romans 10:17 that "faith comes from hearing the message, and the message is heard through the word about Christ." Did you catch that? Faith comes from hearing and knowing God's Word. So let's consider a few things about God's Word.

1. God's Word Is Our Food.

When Satan tempts Jesus in the desert, Jesus reminds us of the power of the Word to sustain us. Jesus was in the hot, dry desert and had been fasting for forty days. He must have been hungry. Knowing this, Satan suggests that Jesus turn some nearby rocks into bread. Jesus' response is fascinating: "Man shall not live on bread alone, but on every word that comes from the mouth of God" (Matthew 4:4). In other words, Jesus was being sustained not by normal food but by spiritual food, the words of God.

Many people see the Bible as a dusty old book with lots of pages and "thou shalts" and "thou shalt nots" that they can't even understand. So they don't read it. And if they grew up in church, they then feel guilty for not reading it. Well, we may indeed feel guilty if we have a habit of not soaking up the Word of God. But more than that, we should feel hungry! God's Word nourishes our soul, the very center of our being. When we deprive our soul of the Word of God, we starve it.

Physical starvation is one of the saddest, most heart-wrenching ways a person can die. I once visited Calcutta, India. I'll never forget walking through the slums and seeing the effects of extreme poverty: the sunken eyes, protruding ribs, and swollen bellies that had not had food in weeks. My heart broke to see little children on the verge of death because they did not have any food.

If you are reading this book, the odds are that you are going to eat today, and you probably have not worried where your next meal will come from. In the West we are physically well fed. I wonder, though, whether many of us have souls that are starving from a serious lack of God's Word. If we could peer into our souls as God can, what would we see? Many of us, I fear, would have shriveled, weak souls. If we could see them, we might feel the way we feel when we see people starving physically. And we would demand that something be given to these poor souls for nourishment.

Thank God for the Bible. Most of us have access to it all day, every day, if only we would take the time to read it. The Bible feeds our souls and strengthens our faith. As we read it, we get a clearer picture of Jesus. Our perspective is improved.

Jesus said that unless we eat his flesh and drink his blood, there is no life in us. Talk about a creepy statement. But understand what Jesus is saying: If we want to experience the real, abundant, eternal life that Jesus offers, the only way is to consume his Word every single day. The same way your body needs food, your soul needs Jesus.

So often we try to live the Christian life without taking in the Word daily. Many of us give in to temptation time and time again because we just are not strong enough to resist. No wonder. When we deprive our souls of what is good, we should not be surprised when we go wrong. When our stomach is empty, we are tempted to fill it with whatever food is nearby, whether or not the food is nutritious. When our soul is empty, we are far more susceptible to temptations to fill that spiritual emptiness with whatever seems good to us in the moment. Sometimes the thing we reach for is good. Sometimes it isn't. A steady diet of Scripture is to the soul what a strictly nutritious diet is to the body.

Fill your soul with the Word of God. Do it every day. You are going to like the result.

2. God's Word Is Our Weapon.

God's Word is our weapon against the enemy. And who is the enemy? Our enemy is the devil, whom Scripture tells us prowls around like a lion seeking people to devour (1 Peter 5:8). Satan probes our defenses, looking to hit us where it will hurt most. We cannot always prevent the attack, but we can prepare for it and be ready to use God's Word in our defense. His Word is a powerful weapon.

> For the word of God is alive and active. Sharper than any double-edged sword, it penetrates even to dividing soul and spirit, joints and marrow; it judges the thoughts and attitudes of the heart.
>
> HEBREWS 4:12

> The sword of the Spirit, which is the word of God.
>
> EPHESIANS 6:17

Notice that Jesus always responded to Satan's temptations in the desert by speaking God's Word. Each time the devil tries to knock Jesus off course, Jesus responds with, "It is written . . ." Jesus knew that even Satan, the embodiment of evil, could not stand against the words of God. It is crucial that we get this. When we face a spiritual attack or an extreme temptation, we can fight back using the Word of God as our weapon. We are not fighting against flesh and blood, but against the rulers, authorities, and powers of this dark world and against spiritual forces of evil in the heavenly realms (Ephesians 6:12). To fight a spiritual battle we need a spiritual weapon.

I was not much of a fighter when I was growing up. I was more of a lover. (At least, that's what I told people when I was too afraid to fight. It sounded better.) But I learned this principle pretty quickly: It's often not about how well you can fight but how well the other person thinks you can fight. So when a fight was coming my way, my plan was to make people think I was crazy. So I would say things like, "Man, you don't know me. I'm crazy! I've been kicked out of three different schools for fighting teachers. You don't want to mess with me, man! I'm off my meds. You don't know me. I'll cut you!"

I know. "I'll cut you"? Who says that? Looking back, it was a silly thing to say. But when Satan tempts us today, it is exactly what we need to say to him!

Devil, you don't know me. You don't know my family. I'm a child of God! I'm the brother of Jesus Christ, the King of kings and Lord of lords, the maker and sustainer of all things, at whose name every knee will bow and every tongue confess. Devil, I'll cut you!

I get fired up just thinking about it! It's like that scene in *Gladiator* where Maximus finally takes off his mask and reveals his identity to the emperor:

My name is Maximus Decimus Meridius, commander of the Armies of the North, General of the Felix Legions, loyal servant to the true emperor, Marcus Aurelius. Father to a murdered son, husband to a murdered wife. And I will have my vengeance, in this life or the next.

God's Word is our weapon and we need to use it!

3. The Word Is Our Guide.

Third, the Word is our guide. It leads, we follow. Many in our generation are desperate for direction. Their lives feel empty, aimless, meaningless. They have bought into the postmodern lie that everything is relative, that we can't really know anything that is really true. Accordingly, they don't really know anything, not even themselves. Every aspect of their lives, such as their decisions about relationships, their friends, and their careers, is based on what feels best at the moment. The longer they make decisions that way, the more empty, lonely, frustrated, and hopeless they feel.

But in God's Word we find the best guide we could ever have. I love what David said in Psalm 119:105: "Your word is a lamp for my feet, a light on my path." What a beautiful picture. In a dark world, when nothing seems certain, when all you can see are shadows, and you are not sure which way to go, the Bible is a light showing the path.

I have a portable GPS in my car. I love it. I just type in the address and it tells me exactly which roads I need to take to get there. It does not matter if I have never been to a particular place before. The GPS is capable of getting me there. And it has different voices to choose from: male, female, American, British. I keep it set on the British lady. I always trust a British accent.

One of the things I love about the GPS is that if I ever

make a wrong turn, it does not stop working. The British lady doesn't call me a "bloody moron" and abandon me. Instead she simply says, "Rerouting" and then gives me new directions. Usually, before I even realize I have strayed from the path, the GPS creates a new route for me and I'm on my way.

Maybe you have gotten off course. Maybe your life is jacked. Maybe your relationships are broken, or your future is in doubt, or your dreams have been crushed. Or maybe you have not quite arrived at any of those places, but you know that you are headed to one of them. Here is what I want you to know: God is pretty great at taking people like you and me and bringing us back to his love, back to his plan, back into his arms.

God's Word will lead you if you will let it. Consume it, fight your battles with it, and follow it as your guide.

> When Jesus heard this, he was amazed at him, and turning to the crowd following him, he said, "I tell you, I have not found such great faith even in Israel." Then the men who had been sent returned to the house and found the servant well.
>
> LUKE 7:9–10

Great faith comes when you decide that his Word is enough.

As we have seen, so much is packed into the centurion's story. This guy had it going on. And yet, in the face of his servant's illness, all the centurion's power, wealth, and influence were worthless. And he was in a crisis. Centurions were hardened, self-reliant individuals, but ultimately this one realized that his abilities only reached so far. In order to save his servant, he would have to go beyond himself. And at the end of himself, the centurion found Jesus.

Part Two

THE WIDOW

Soon afterward, Jesus went to a town called Nain, and his
disciples and a large crowd went along with him. As he
approached the town gate, a dead person was being carried
out—the only son of his mother, and she was a widow. And
a large crowd from the town was with her. When the Lord
saw her, his heart went out to her and he said, "Don't cry."
Then he went up and touched the bier they were carrying
him on, and the bearers stood still. He said, "Young man,
I say to you, get up!" The dead man sat up and began
to talk, and Jesus gave him back to his mother.
They were all filled with awe and praised God. "A great
prophet has appeared among us," they said. "God has
come to help his people." This news about Jesus spread
throughout Judea and the surrounding country.

LUKE 7:11–17

Chapter Four

A TOWN CALLED NAIN

Soon afterward, Jesus went to a town called Nain, and
his disciples and a large crowd went along with him. As
he approached the town gate, a dead person was being
carried out—the only son of his mother, and she was a
widow. And a large crowd from the town was with her.

LUKE 7:11–12

It's Not You. It's Me.

Have you ever been dumped? I have, plenty of times. It's the worst. You date someone for a few weeks or months or years. You put everything you have into the relationship—time, feelings, money—only to find out that what you thought you had with that other person was an illusion. You were making it up.

Out of nowhere, your soon-to-be-ex says, "I just want to be friends," or "I need to focus on my career right now," or "It's not you. It's me." Please. If I were Ryan Gosling, I bet the "me" who said that would not have broken it off. My all-time favorite line—only church people say this—is: "I just feel like God wants us to break up." Wait, what? Are *you* breaking up with me or is God? I talked to him this morning and he didn't mention anything about it.

Breakups have been around as long as relationships. We even see a few examples in the Bible. You didn't know the Bible dealt with breakups? Here are just two examples.

A prophet named Hosea buys a slave girl and marries her. She then leaves Hosea and becomes a prostitute. It's a bad day when your wife says, "I'm out of here. I'd rather be a hooker than be married to you!" Ouch.

Samson's girlfriend puts him to sleep with the ancient equivalent of NyQuil, then shaves his head while he's knocked out. She then wakes him up to tell him that he has been sold to his enemy. Anyone ever been dumped with the line, "It's not you. It's your hair"? Me either.

Dumped on Thanksgiving

I have been married for nine incredible years, and my wife is amazing, like seriously amazing. Most days I have no idea how I could be so lucky that I got to marry her. She is crazy talented, super fun, smart, warm, caring. She is also my best friend.

We met when we were seventeen. I was in Nashville visiting my older brother, Jonfulton. He was touring with his band and performing at a school. I was sitting in the auditorium during the sound check when I looked up to the top row and saw her, DawnCheré Lynea Duron. Everything else in the room stopped. I was looking at an angel coming down from heaven. That's a cliché, I know, but you weren't there. I was on the floor of the auditorium and she was in the back row, way above me. The light shined behind her and lit up her blonde hair, almost like a halo. I may or may not have heard the "Hallelujah Chorus," but it was love at first sight. As soon as I saw her I said in my mind, "I choose you."

I wish I could say that DawnCheré saw me and immediately chose me too, but it took a long time and a lot of convincing. I eventually wore her down. First we became great friends and discovered that we had a lot in common—parents in the ministry, love of music, passion for God. And the differences attracted us more to each other. Before long we were inseparable. We dated throughout college and did everything together—school, friends, family, ministry.

But our relationship was not perfect. DawnCheré broke up with me more than once. And each time it hurt. A whole lot. One thing you need to know about me is that I'm not a drama queen. I'm a drama king. My mom would tell people, "Richie feels deeply." I think that was her nice way of saying that I'm borderline emotionally unstable. There is a space between "he cries easily" and "maybe we should have him committed to an asylum." I live in that space.

One Thanksgiving, DawnCheré broke up with me. I was crushed. I was at home, and my churchy family was celebrating with an awesome feast and singing hymns.

> Give thanks with a grateful heart;
> Give thanks to the Holy One.
> Give thanks because He's given
> Jesus Christ, His Son.

I didn't eat anything all day. Do you know how sad a person must be not to eat Thanksgiving dinner? No turkey. No dressing. No pie. I just moped around the house and sang my own hymns as I choked on my own tears:

> Give thanks with a broken heart;
> Give thanks for this heartless girl.
> Give thanks because she's stolen
> All my joy in the world.

Joking aside, when DawnCheré—my best friend, my love, the person I would one day marry—broke up with me, I was forced to answer some serious questions. Was DawnCheré the source of my joy and peace? Had I put my hope in her? Was my satisfaction, my completion, my wholeness dependent on another person? Was Jesus my foundation, as I had thought, or was my life built on my relationship with DawnCheré? It took a few months, but DawnCheré and I eventually worked out our differences and got engaged and were married three years later.

Intentionally or not, many of us build our lives on other people in one way or another. We may depend on them emotionally or see them as our happiness, our peace, or our strength. We may literally feel that we cannot live without them. Now, I'm not suggesting that relationships are evil or that you should cut off all contact with people and go live in a cave. What I want to point out is that relationships are fragile. They are fragile because people are fragile. If we build our lives on a fragile foundation, on some kind of sand, the foundation will eventually crack and the life we have built will fall apart. Maybe not your whole life, but a good bit of it.

A Town Called Nain

After Jesus healed the centurion's servant, he left Capernaum and headed to Nain, a town with an interesting name. "Nain" usually means "pasture," but it can also mean "beautiful" or "afflicted." Beautiful and afflicted. Isn't that a strange contradiction?

Well, it is a contradiction, but it is one that most people are familiar with when they think about it. In fact, there may be no better description of humanity than "beautiful and afflicted." We are created in the image of God Almighty, and we exhibit tremendous beauty as a result. We love, we create, we care. But we are also capable of tremendous evil. For all the wonderful things we humans do, there is something inside holding us back, an affliction that prevents us from being all we were created to be. We call that affliction "sin," and it is responsible for all of the pain and suffering we see every day.

Nain—beautiful and afflicted—was roughly twenty-five miles from Capernaum. Jesus and his crowd are heading to Nain on a high note. Jesus has been healing people left and right. He has just healed the centurion's servant in Capernaum, and before that he had preached the greatest sermon, the Sermon on the Mount. His fame is swelling. His followers know that they are in on something special. Their excitement is palpable. People are giving thanks for the blessings that God is pouring out through Jesus. They are full of joy, probably laughing as they recount the amazing things Jesus has been doing.

"Did you see the guy with the shriveled hand? All cracked and oozing. Gross! He hadn't used that thing in years. And Jesus just said, 'Stretch out your hand,' and he did and got healed!"

"I know! What about that guy with leprosy, with the skin falling off his face? Jesus actually touched that guy. I couldn't believe it. And he said, 'Be clean,' and immediately the leprosy was gone! It was ridiculous!"

"And what about that guy on the bed, remember, the paralyzed guy whose friends tore off that roof and lowered him down with ropes? How crazy was that? There's no way the homeowner's insurance is paying for that."

As Jesus' group gets close to the city gate, a different crowd is leaving Nain. This one is different than the jubilant, celebratory crowd surrounding Jesus. It is somber and quiet. Eyes downcast, the group moves slowly. People are crying. This is a funeral procession.

Isn't it just like the Bible to give us this paradox, to put these two groups side by side, one celebrating God's healing power and one mourning the death of a loved one? Just outside Nain, the beautiful and afflicted place, we see a beautiful group walking into the city and an afflicted group walking out.

Life can be like that. When one side is winning, the other is losing. One of your friends is getting married. Another is getting divorced. A baby is born. A loved one dies. That is the scene outside Nain as Jesus and his followers arrive.

A young man has died and some people from the town, including his mother, are carrying his body out of the city to be buried. The mother is weeping, and rightfully so. Not only has she lost her beloved son, she was a widow. She had lost her partner, her love, her protector and provider. For a woman living in that culture, losing her husband was a massive blow. Aside from the emotional torment of losing a spouse, her breadwinner was gone. And yet she still had hope, because her son would care for her. He would provide. He might not meet the emotional needs that her husband had met, but she would not have to live on the street. Her son was her future, her legacy, her insurance plan. Whatever happiness she still had depended on him. In the midst of the darkness after her husband died, a faint light flickered in the form of her son. And now he was dead. Her future, her plan, dead.

A Rude Awakening

When I was a senior in college, I traveled from Tennessee to California to visit some friends. A few days after my arrival, my phone rang. It was my mom and she sounded worried. She told me that she was on her way to Sacramento, where her brother had just been admitted to the hospital. She said it was serious, maybe cancer, and she asked that I meet her there. I jumped on the next flight from Los Angeles. I left behind good friends and great times and made my way to my uncle, who had been hospitalized with who knew what. It was a surreal flight. My uncle was one of the most powerful men I had known. His personality was electric. He was physically strong and fit. He had a beautiful family and a multimillion dollar business. He had everything he ever wanted. In my eyes nothing was stronger than he was. Now I sat on a plane wondering if he had cancer.

When I arrived in Sacramento, my aunt picked me up and drove me directly to the hospital. My uncle had been admitted just days before, but his condition had worsened drastically since then. The next few days were a blur. The doctor confirmed that my uncle had stage 4 lung cancer. The strong, powerful man I knew and loved was wasting away. I remember the doctor gathering the whole family in the waiting room to say, "At this point we're not talking about quantity of time. It's more about quality of time." My uncle was not going to make it. The only thing we and the doctors could do was to help him die in peace. Up until that point, in spite of what I had seen, I still believed that my uncle would pull through. He was so strong, after all, so full of life. Surely he had more time. But when the doctor spoke, things got real.

That night I stayed with my uncle in his hospital room. We were awake all night. He had to drink a gallon of a disgusting liquid for a test the next morning. Every hour or so I helped him into the bathroom. For a twenty-year-old kid who had never seen cancer firsthand, it was a rude awakening.

Between sips of medical solution and trips to the restroom, my uncle and I talked. We spoke about family, about life, about all the important things a man thinks about on his deathbed. There is something about dire circumstances that forces people to get real with each other. I guess that when you lose your health and some of your dignity, there is really no point in wearing a mask anymore. I stayed for two more days and then headed back home. My uncle passed away about a month later. I still miss him.

Life is fragile. People are mortal. It does not matter who you are. It does not matter how well you take care of yourself. One call from the doctor can change everything.

THE PROBLEM

Look, our relationships can be some of the most wonderful things. Friendship is beautiful. It is crucial. Our friends celebrate our greatest victories with us, and they encourage us through our greatest challenges. Romantic love is amazing. It is one of the things that makes life worth living. Love between parents and children is phenomenal, inspiring. These things are absolutely necessary. They were created by God for our good and for his glory.

But sometimes we worship the creation instead of the Creator. It is possible to love someone in such a way that it becomes sinful. You can hold a person in such high regard that your treatment of that person is not actually love; it is idolatry. When your love turns into worship of that person, you have taken a wrong turn. You are giving glory to a person when it should be given to God.

Idolizing another person is unfair to them and dangerous to you. It's unfair because humans were not meant to be worshiped. We are worshipers, not worshipees. And when we receive worship, all sorts of bad spiritual consequences occur. We become proud. We lose the ability to hear and receive correction. We become arrogant, stubborn, foolish, and eventually, we fall.

Idolizing a person is dangerous because people are not perfect. Even without the added pressure and temptation of being worshiped, people mess up all the time. But give a person the extra burden of carrying your hopes and dreams and you are bound to get disappointed. People cannot carry that weight. They were not meant to.

Now hear me on this. It is one thing to support, encourage, and believe in someone. Those are good things, godly things. But it is quite another thing to put your *hope* in another person. God is our hope, not people. People will fail us, reject us, or betray us. And when they do, the consequences can be devastating—emotionally, relationally, spiritually. People are amazing, but they make terrible gods.

In his book *The Great Divorce*, C. S. Lewis tells a heartbreaking story about a mother who worshiped her son. She doted on him every minute. She cared for him, loved him, provided for him. Her whole life was devoted to him. In her eyes (and in many people's eyes), her love toward her son was appropriate. She was a mother, after all, and aren't mothers supposed to put their children first? She did not see that although a mother's self-sacrifice for her child is right and good, placing that child at the top of her list of priorities was sinful. She believed that loving her son was the most important thing in the world, and she failed to recognize that her love for her son prevented her from knowing what is best in the world: God.

In the story, the woman meets her brother, Reginald, just outside of heaven. Reginald is focused on making sure the woman makes it into heaven, but the woman is not concerned with heaven at all. She is far more worried about when and where she will see her son:

> "If He loved me He'd let me see my boy. If He loved me why did He take Michael away from me? I wasn't going to say anything about that. But it's pretty hard to forgive, you know."
>
> "But He had to take Michael away. Partly for Michael's sake . . ."
>
> "I'm sure I did my best to make Michael happy. I gave up my whole life . . ."
>
> "Human beings can't make one another really happy for long. And secondly, for your sake. He wanted your merely instinctive love for your child (tigresses share that, you know!) to turn into something better. He wanted you to love Michael as He understands love. You cannot love a fellow-creature fully till you love God. Sometimes this conversion can be

done while the instinctive love is still gratified. But there was, it seems, no chance of that in your case. The instinct was uncontrolled and fierce and monomaniac. (Ask your daughter, or your husband. Ask your own mother. You haven't once thought of her.) The only remedy was to take away its object. It was a case for surgery. When that first kind of love was thwarted, then there was just a chance that in the loneliness, in the silence, something else might begin to grow."

"This is all nonsense—cruel and wicked nonsense. What right have you to say things like that about Mother-love? It is the highest and holiest feeling in human nature."

"Pam, Pam—no natural feelings are high or low, holy or unholy, in themselves. They are all holy when God's hand is on the rein. They all go bad when they set up on their own and make themselves into false gods."

It is so tempting to buy into the lie that another person can make us whole. No shortage of movies, songs, and advertisements shout that lie at us every day. It would be convenient if life were like that scene in *Jerry Maguire* where Tom Cruise comes busting into the house, looks at Renée Zellweger, and says that famous line, "You complete me!" And we would live happily ever after (at least until Tom starts jumping on Oprah's couch and shouting nonsense on national television—that's kind of awkward).

People can treat love and marriage this way. They think the fairy tales are true. If they could find Prince Charming or convince the princess to be with them, everything would just magically fall into place and they would live happily ever after.

Now, fairy tales are great. But there is a reason they are so captivating. They're fiction. In real life, "happily ever after" is not automatic. Great relationships and "fairy tale" marriages are possible, but they take hard work. They take sacrifice, humility, and lots and lots of grace.

But you will not be "completed" by another person. You are a whole person, but God created you to need relationships. Remember that "it is not good for the man to be alone" thing from Genesis 2:18? God knew that we needed relationships with other people and a relationship with him. But the other people—family, friends, spouse—do not complete you. They complement you. And in your relationships, your love for others reflects the love that God has for his Son, Jesus. This is how human relationships were meant to be: mutual love between two people reflecting the mutual love between God the Father and Jesus the Son.

When we worship another person instead of loving him or her the way God intended, we get let down, betrayed, hurt. Allowing our hope to rest on another person eventually leaves us relationally and emotionally bankrupt.

TOO LATE

You may have been down this road already. You may have placed your hope in another person, perhaps a boyfriend, a girlfriend, a spouse, a sibling, a friend, a parent, a teacher, a coach, or even a pastor. Whoever it was, that person may have let you down, big time. Your plans didn't work out the way you hoped they would. Maybe it was worse than that. Your future, the one that was more real to you than your present, was shattered and ripped away from you. It crushed you and hurt you deeply. You grieved or became angry or cursed. Maybe you were so upset that you did not even eat any pie on Thanksgiving Day! On the outside you held it together, but on the inside you were broken and in pain. And maybe you stayed in that place, refusing to get burned again. You held it together on the outside, but on the inside it was agony. Your heart hardened. You became cold toward others. Better not to trust at all, you thought, than to trust and get crushed again.

If you are not careful you may find yourself living in the Nain of affliction forever. You can fool everyone else into believing you are fine, but you know better. You know that things might look fine on the outside, but your heart is a mess. Your tears blur your vision. You can't see past your pain. If that is you or someone you know, here is what I want you to know: You don't have to stay in the Nain of affliction.

Leaving Nain

Many of us are living with pain that we never were meant to live with. The purpose of physical pain is to warn us that something is not right and to let us know that we need to get to safety as fast as possible. When you put your hand on a hot stove, the pain signals "take your hand off!" before it gets any worse. When you have a severe headache that won't go away, that is a signal to see a doctor. Whether or not you actually go to see a doctor is up to you, but the pain did its job. It let you know something was wrong.

Emotional pain is just as real, and sometimes much worse, than physical pain. It is a signal that something has gone wrong, typically in a relationship—with a father, mother, significant other, close friend. When you experience emotional pain, you have a choice. You can deal with whatever is causing it or just live with it. Unfortunately, when it comes to emotional pain many of us choose to live with it. We feel the stove burning our hand but we don't move our hand. And the pain keeps getting worse, and the burden of living with it gets heavier. Before long you are dragging that burden everywhere. It affects your attitude. It weighs down your other relationships, which results in more pain, which turns into more weight, and the cycle continues. Maybe it is time to leave Nain.

A WOUND THAT IS NEGLECTED GETS INFECTED

Once when I was a kid and my parents were out of town, my older brother and I were staying with a friend. We decided to play something we called "bike tag." Bike tag is similar to regular tag, only, you guessed it, everyone is on a bike. So there we were, a bunch of nine-year-old boys riding bikes full speed toward one another in the street trying to reach out and tag anyone nearby. What could possibly go wrong?

A friend and I were behind a parked car, hiding from my brother. He was "it." It didn't take long before "it" found us, and my friend panicked. We were side by side on our bikes, and when he gave his kickstand a swift heel-kick, that metal stand sliced deep into my leg. I started bleeding all over the place.

Friends rushed me inside, where someone's mom washed the cut as well as she could. The bleeding eventually stopped, but the cut was long and deep and needed stitches. Never mind. I just put a bandage on it and went back outside. Three days later the cut got infected. Ooze, pus, the whole nine yards.

One of the worst mistakes we can make when it comes to emotional pain is to ignore it, the way I ignored my kickstand cut. Just like you should not leave your hand on a hot stove, when you experience emotional pain you have to deal with whatever is causing it. Ignoring it will not make it go away. It will only get worse.

You might be able to distract yourself for a while, and people try all the time. Our world is ready to sell you all kinds of distractions—alcohol, drugs, entertainment, sex. But those only treat the symptom, not the cause. Alcohol can deaden your pain for a while. A funny movie, a good song, or a ball-game can take your mind off of the pain for a while. But only for a while. At the end of the day, when the distractions end, when the drugs have worn off, when it is just you and reality, the pain is still there. There is a reason it is still there. You have not dealt with whatever is causing it.

How you deal with your emotional pain will depend on your circumstances, but from what I have seen, there is at least one thing that helps in every case. Talking to someone. As simple as it sounds, and as awkward as it might be, telling another person about the pain is one of the best ways to deal with it. When you experience emotional pain, don't carry that weight alone. Let the people who love you help. If you don't, it's going to get worse.

PLAYING HURT

Wounded does not mean dead. But sometimes the pain is so intense we don't care. The widow in the Nain story was not dead, but she probably felt as if she was. Sometimes we are hurt so deeply, the wound so painful, it feels like we will never escape. It feels like we will never smile or laugh again. It feels like life as we knew it is over. I get it. I've been there. But having been there, let me assure you: Life is not over.

During my short-lived football career, I injured my thumb pretty badly. I was making a tackle and my hand got caught on a helmet. The helmet went one way, I went the other way, and my thumb went with the helmet. It didn't quite come off, but, man, it sure felt like it did. I grabbed it, popped it back into place, and ran straight for the sidelines, certain I was finished for the game. My whole hand was throbbing. I showed my coach and told him I couldn't keep playing. He grabbed my wrist, surveyed the damage, and then instead of sending me to the trainer he slapped my hand and yelled, "Get back on the field, Wilkerson!" I didn't think there was any way I could play, but I marched back out there and got into position. On the next play I intercepted a long pass. It was the highlight of my brief, but brilliant, football career. If I had not stayed in the game, I would have missed out on my one highlight.

We may think that the wound is holding us back, but it is not the wound holding us back. It is the *belief* that the wound is holding us back. There is power in belief. Often, in order to take that first step out of Nain, we just have to suck it up and move forward. We have to march ourselves back out onto

the field of life and get ready for the next play. You won't feel
like moving forward, but sometimes that is exactly what you
have to do.

Tell yourself that you do not have to stay in Nain. Say it
out loud. Say it until you start to believe it. You will be amazed
where you can go if you believe you can get there.

Time Helps, but Jesus Heals

If you are serious about getting out of Nain, I know someone
who can help. In fact, he is the only one who knows the way.
Actually, he *is* the way. You can take the right steps. You can
follow the right advice, but in order to find the ultimate peace
and joy that you are looking for, you need Jesus. Friends help.
Belief helps. Time helps. But Jesus heals.

The Bible says that God is close to the brokenhearted and
saves those who are crushed in spirit. He specializes in fixing
broken lives. In fact, brokenness is a prerequisite to knowing
God. After all, it is hard to fix something that is not broken,
isn't it?

One of the things I love about Jesus is simply that he
understands us. His own heart was broken. He was betrayed
by one of his disciples, rejected by almost all of the people he
came to save, and plagued with temptations in all the ways we
are. Hebrews 4:15 says, "For we do not have a high priest who
is unable to empathize with our weaknesses, but we have one
who has been tempted in every way, just as we are—yet he did
not sin."

Jesus was tempted. He knows what it's like. He knows

your pain, and not just on an intellectual level. He doesn't just know *about* your pain. He *knows* your pain. He experienced it himself. He knows exactly how you feel, and on the cross he spread out his arms to show you just how much he loves you. With all your wounds, in all your pain, Jesus loves you, and he wants to help you out of Nain. He wants to help you get rid of that affliction—sin—that is holding you back. He wants to get you out of Nain and take you to places you never dreamed were possible.

The Widow

The widow in Nain was in a terrible place. The two most important people in her life, her husband and her son, were dead. Her dreams were shattered. Even her backup plan had been ruined. With her son gone she, too, was almost as good as dead. Everything she held dear was gone. She seemed to be without hope, bankrupt.

But what the widow did not know was that her only son was about to meet God's only Son. One was alive and destined to die. The other was dead but destined to live. What happened next is one of the most amazing things in the Bible.

Chapter Five

DON'T CRY

When the Lord saw her, his heart went out to her and he said, "Don't cry." Then he went up and touched the bier they were carrying him on, and the bearers stood still. He said, "Young man, I say to you, get up!" The dead man sat up and began to talk, and Jesus gave him back to his mother.

LUKE 7:13–15

The Savior's Setup

As the widow and the funeral party are leaving the city, notice that Jesus is just arriving. Jesus' timing is important and often overlooked. He shows up at just the right moment. Is this a coincidence? I don't think so. I think this is an example of what I like to call the "Savior's setup." I mean, what are the chances of Jesus showing up exactly as the dead son is being carried on the bier? Fifteen minutes earlier or fifteen minutes later and Jesus would have missed them. But he showed up precisely in time to cross the widow's path. He set up the circumstances perfectly in order to do a great work in the widow's life at just the right time.

Let me tell you something about Jesus. He is never late. He is always right on time. Jesus shows up exactly when we need him to show up. I know that is tough to believe. We live in a world that promises to be "on time" but often lets us down. And, as usual, we let that experience influence our understanding of God.

I fly a lot. I love the traveling but I am not a big fan of flying. Well, the actual flying is okay. It is the part before and after being in the air that bothers me. What frustrates me most is that airlines don't ever just cancel a flight right away. Instead, they toy with you. They wait until about five minutes before the scheduled departure time and then they say, "Attention ladies and gentlemen: Flight 57 has been delayed for thirty minutes" (just to give you hope). Then they do this three or four more times until they finally cancel it.

I was once delayed for an hour and a half, but by some miraculous grace, we arrived at our destination on time! As I was walking off the plane, I asked a flight attendant how we arrived on time. "Well, the pilot just flew faster," she said. Wait, what? Planes can fly faster? When they leave late, then why don't they go faster all the time, to arrive on time? Is there some sort of above-the-clouds speed limit I am not aware of? This kind of thing makes people assume the worst about airlines. People think if there is a delay the flight will be canceled. Or if their bags are not the first ones onto the carousel they are probably lost forever. Or if there is turbulence the plane is going down.

Some of us think Jesus is like an airline company, promising one thing but failing to deliver.

I mentioned at the start of the book that I was fourteen years old when my family moved from Tacoma to Miami, and that there were many cultural differences between the two cities, as well as big differences in the weather (in Miami it can be rainy and sunny at the same time) and the food (before Miami, I never knew beans and rice existed). And boy, were the people ever different in Miami.

Take, for example, the first wedding I attended there. It was for a Haitian man and a Puerto Rican woman. The invitation said the wedding would take place on a particular Saturday at 4 P.M. In Tacoma, that meant arriving at 3:45 (at the latest), because the wedding would start at four sharp. At the Puerto Rican and Haitian wedding, I learned the meaning of the suffix "ish," as in "the wedding will be on Saturday at 4(ish)."

I showed up as I normally do, fifteen minutes early, looking forward to a lovely wedding, a quick reception, and getting home in time for the prime-time Nickelodeon shows. I chose a seat, sat down, and waited. Four o'clock came and went. It made me anxious. I had never been to a wedding that did not start on time. I figured something was wrong. An hour went by, and I asked my mom, "I guess there's no wedding today, huh?" The guy next to me said, "Hold on. Everything is fine. Don't leave too soon." We waited some more. Two hours later the wedding began. And let me tell you, it was worth the wait. Once things started, there was no chance I was going to get home in time for any TV shows. The wedding was beautiful and the party afterward went on and on and on. I got home shortly before the sun came up the next morning.

When it comes to timing, sometimes Jesus is like that wedding. He may show up later than you expect, but he is going to show up, and once he does, you will be better than you ever could have guessed. You might be delayed, but you are not denied. You are not defeated. You are not destroyed.

RIGHT THING, WRONG TIME

We are impatient people. It is a symptom of our sinful nature. We are all about "me" most of the time, so when we want something we want it immediately. That is why some of us stare a hole through the microwave while the popcorn is popping. It is why we get frustrated when that thing we ordered online takes more than two days to arrive. When we want something, we think the right time is right now. But "right now" is not always the right time. In fact, getting the right thing at the wrong time can present problems we never expected.

For example, have you ever watched one of those documentaries on TV about people who won the lottery? Holy smokes. In most of the stories, those people end up way worse off than they were before they won. Of course they are thrilled at first. They got exactly what they wanted when they wanted it. And then they start buying everything their heart desires. They don't have to work for it. They don't have to earn it. They can have whatever they want immediately. You would think they would be so happy. But often, the money ruins the things that had been most valuable to them. Their loved ones become envious. Their kids become greedy. They can't tell their genuine friends apart from people that just want something from them. They have an accidental empire that they now have to manage but they lack the tools to manage it. Before long, things falls apart. The kids leave. The marriage ends. Friendships are lost. And the lottery winner may turn to drugs or alcohol to deaden the pain. It's tragic. It's not that the money is bad in and of itself. Rather, people got a good thing at the wrong time.

Some of the things we desire are not wrong, but "right now" is not the right time. Timing is everything and our job is to learn to trust God's timing even when we would rather have our desire met right now. His timing is always better than our timing.

I love how Paul says it in Romans 5:6: "You see, at just the right time, when we were still powerless, Christ died for the ungodly."

When we were "powerless," Jesus gave his very life on our behalf. He loved us that much. We were unable to do anything for him. We could not even love him. At our lowest moment, he did his greatest work. When we were on our worst behavior, Jesus was on his best behavior. He came for us at just the right time.

I love this one too: "And we know that in all things God works for the good of those who love him, who have been called according to his purpose" (Romans 8:28). In *all things* God works for the good of those who love him. Not in some things. In all things. All circumstances. All events. All celebrations. All frustrations. All trials. All victories. All defeats. In all things God is working for the good of those who love him. For believers this means that when you did not get what you wanted when you wanted it, it is because God knew that there was something better for you. Either what you desired was not the right thing or it was not the right time for it. Either way, God is looking out for your good. Not just that, God is working *everything* together, like a puzzle, for your good. Wow!

DON'T CRY. HE ISN'T LATE.

Can you imagine what God's timing for the widow in our story must have been like? Your husband is dead. Now your son has died. Your life as you know it is over. So you're now holding the funeral for your beloved son, and as his body is being carried out of the city for burial, you are stopped by a man you have never met. He seems friendly, and you can tell he hurts for you. "That's nice," you think, "but let me move on and bury my son, please."

Then he says something that cuts you to the core: "Don't cry."

"Don't what? Don't cry? Don't you realize what is going on? Can't you see that my son is dead? And by the way, so is my husband! *Don't cry?* My life is over! And where is God when I needed him? Where was he when I was on my knees praying for him to spare my son's life? Didn't he hear me? Where was God when he died?"

But Jesus' "don't cry" is not meant to offend the widow. It is meant to give her hope. Jesus is saying something like, "Don't cry. God isn't late. His timing is perfect."

Then Jesus walks over to the bier and says, "Young man, I say to you, get up!" And the son sits up and begins to talk. Did you get that? Jesus brought a dead guy back to life!

I don't know what is going on in your life. I don't know what problems you have or what you desire from God at the moment. But I know this: God is never late. His timing is always perfect. And your situation may seem hopeless. You may think that there is no way out, that there is no way even God could help you now. You may be frustrated that he has not answered your prayers. Know this: if God can answer a widow's prayer to heal her son *after the son has died*, he can also give you exactly what you need at exactly the right time. It might not be right now, but it will be at the right time.

Christian Cusswords

As a child I had a small speech impediment. I was not able to make the "s" sound properly. It always came out as the "f" sound. This was frustrating because people did not always understand what I was trying to say.

When I was about six years old there was this bully on my block who was always messing with me. Really tough. A lot bigger than I was. And mean. Big, bad, and ugly. Constantly making fun of me and pushing me around. Her name was Christina. (I know. I'm still embarrassed by it.)

Now, in my house we were not allowed to say certain words. In fact those words were considered like cusswords, and in the Wilkerson house you'd better not get caught saying them. They were like the pastor's version of cusswords— Christian cusswords. One of those Christian cusswords was "shut up."

One day, the big, bad, ugly bully Christian-cussed me out. She told me I was stupid and needed to shut up. I remember running into the house and crying to my dad.

"Dad, Chriftina fed 'fut up.'"

"What son?"

"Chriftina fed 'fut up,' Dad!"

"Son, I don't understand what you're saying."

"Dad, I'm telling you: Chriftina fed 'fut up'! Fee'f a finner, Dad, fee'f a finner. Fee fed 'fut up'!"

No matter how hard I tried to explain it, my pronunciations just did not suffice. I was trying to tell my dad that Christina said "shut up" and so she was a sinner. In my six-year-old pastor's-kid mind, the worst thing I could call someone was a "sinner." I wanted my dad to know that this girl was in need of the saving grace of Jesus Christ, or, if she did not want that, she could just go to hell like she deserved. (What do you want from me? I was six.)

Another time, my speech impediment landed me in some hot trouble. One Saturday, my family and I went to get a haircut. I hated haircuts when I was little, but our barber had a deal with us. If we did not cry during the haircut, he would give us a lollipop at the end. Actually, where I grew up, we didn't call them "lollipops." We called them "suckers." You can guess where this is going.

I remember that day so vividly. I desperately wanted a sucker. I sat absolutely still and didn't make a sound until the haircut was over. As the barber finished, he asked, "Who wants a sucker?"

With everything in me I shouted out, "I WANT A . . ."— and then my speech impediment kicked in. What a scene. The pastor's kid was shouting what people thought was the F-word. The older men in the shop were getting upset. The pastor was yelling at his kid to shut up. The barber was laughing hysterically. It was bad. I never got a sucker that day. Why? Because in the world, we don't get things when we don't ask for them the right way. Obviously, the way I asked for the sucker was way off.

Christians often apply a similar rule. We say our prayers, thinking that if we ask for something in just the right way, with just the right words, God will give us what we want. But God is not swayed because our words impress him. God is so good and so big and so wise that he gives us what we need, whether we use the right words or not. Sometimes he gives us what we need even without our asking for it.

The widow never asked for Jesus' help. Jesus just showed up and raised her son back to life. She didn't ask. She didn't plead. She didn't beg. She didn't write out a long speech with big words. For all we know she didn't even look at Jesus until he approached her. God is for us, and Jesus, the embodiment of grace, is working all things together for the good of those who love him, whether they ask for it or not.

His Heart Went out to Her

Notice also in our story that before Jesus tells the widow not to cry, "his heart went out to her." In other words, Jesus pitied the widow. He hurt for her.

That short sentence from the text tells us so much about Jesus. It is evidence that Jesus cares about our feelings. It tells us that Jesus does not like to see people in pain. Death breaks Jesus' heart. It actually hurts him. He knows that when God first made the world, it was good. Sin corrupted God's good world and introduced death and all the pain that goes with it. Jesus knows how amazing the world would be if people turned away from sin and back to God.

Sometimes in our churches we are encouraged to hide our pain. Even when we are hurting we are encouraged to smile, to "fake it until we make it." As long as I keep that smile on, I'm walking in faith. Well, a positive attitude is a good thing, and great faith in God is an awesome thing. But if we are covering up our pain and putting on a happy face because we think that is the proper behavior, or because we believe that God does not care about our feelings, we're wrong. Our feelings are a big deal to God. Jesus cares about how we feel. In fact, when we feel, Jesus feels. When we experience sorrow, he feels it too. His heart goes out to us. When we feel glad, he feels that too.

Many translations of Luke 7:13 say that Jesus "had compassion" on the widow. I love the word *compassion*. It means a feeling of sorrow followed by a deep desire to alleviate suffering. Isn't that amazing? Jesus Christ sees our pain and experiences our sorrow and has a deep desire to alleviate our suffering. Most of us experience sympathy when we see others in pain. For most of us, when we see a bad situation it makes our hearts hurt. We see starving children or abused animals on TV and we feel sorry for them. We might even shed a tear or two. That is sympathy. Sympathy is nice, but it usually does not lead to doing much to alleviate the suffering. When was the last time you made a donation to help alleviate the plight of starving children, or volunteered your time, or did anything to help?

The difference between sympathy and compassion is action. And the Bible tells us that Jesus had compassion on the widow. He felt bad for her, but he did not just feel bad for her. When he says, "don't cry," it is because he is about to give her a reason to rejoice. He is going to do what is impossible for her to do. It is as if he is saying, "Don't cry. I love you more than you could possibly know. And what I have in store for you is beyond your wildest imagination."

Don't cry. Jesus loves you. He loves you with a love that is bigger than most of us understand. In fact, the English language does not even have a word for this kind of love. But the Greek language does.

Four Loves

Love. It's an interesting word. Is there another word in our language that carries so much significance? Is there another word that can express such a broad range of feelings? We use the word *love* in a hundred different ways. I love my wife. I love my mom. I love my friends. I love the Seattle Seahawks. I love hamburgers. I love hip hop music. I love my country. In all of these examples the word *love* always conveys something positive, but the "something positive" is different in each case.

Now, because you speak English and because you and I share a culture, you pretty much understand what I mean when I say that I love my wife and that I love hamburgers. You understand that I don't I feel the same way about hamburgers as I feel about DawnCheré, but for whatever reason we use the same word, *love*, in both cases. In the Greek language, however, the language in which the New Testament was written, there are at least four different words that we translate into the English word *love*. They are *storge, philia, eros,* and *agape.* C. S. Lewis beautifully describes the unique meaning of each one of these different types of love in his book *The Four Loves.* And to understand how Jesus loves, we need to take a look at each one.

Storge

Storge love is a natural affection for someone or something. It is love that members of a family feel for one another. A mother's love for her newborn baby is storge love. The love that people feel for their pets is storge love. It is almost an innate or default love. We feel storge love simply because we are in a particular relationship with something or someone, usually a family member. Whatever happens, we love our family. We may not always like them, but we are loyal to them. We want what is good for them. We have natural affection for them. This is storge.

Philia

Philia love is the love that friends have for one another. It is the way that you and your best friend feel about each other. It is a strong bond based on shared experiences, mutual respect, and affection. You both have things in common and care for one another, look out for one another. You choose to spend time together. That's philia.

Eros

I should not even have to discuss eros love. It is where we get our English word *erotic*. And our culture is obsessed with it. Virtually every movie, song, and advertisement pays homage to eros. Eros is romantic love. It is the passionate feeling between a man and a woman. It is the butterflies in your stomach when your beloved walks into the room. It is what we sometimes call "chemistry."

Agape

Agape love is completely different from the first three, which are all different kinds of feelings. I feel affection for my family. I feel a bond with my best friend. I feel attracted to my wife. But agape love is not a feeling. Agape love is all about action. Agape love is a commitment to work for the good of another person. It is a choice. It has nothing to do with feelings, and it has nothing to do with whether or not the other person deserves the help. The closest English word we have is charity. But when we hear the word *charity*, we think of organizations such as the Salvation Army and the United Way, which provide help to needy people. That is not what I mean by charity. Charity means helping regardless of whether the help is deserved. This is agape love. It is unconditional help. And when the Bible talks about Jesus' love for us, it uses the word *agape* to describe that love. Jesus is the embodiment of unconditional love. He is agape.

The apostle Paul gives us a great illustration of what agape love looks like:

> Love is patient, love is kind. It does not envy, it does not boast, it is not proud. It does not dishonor others, it is not self-seeking, it is not easily angered, it keeps no record of wrongs. Love does not delight in evil but rejoices with the truth. It always protects, always trusts, always hopes, always perseveres.
>
> 1 Corinthians 13:4–7

You want to know what true love looks like? Read 1 Corinthians 13. It is patient. It is kind. It is humble. It works for someone else's good. It forgives. It never quits. This kind of love has nothing to do with chemistry or whether or not the other person deserves to be loved this way. It is a choice. It is a habit. It is a virtue. It is the highest virtue.

All of us want to be loved. And if we're honest, we want more than the first three kinds of love provide. Storge love—affection from our family—is wonderful, but it is not enough. Philia—love between friends—is powerful, and it is a huge blessing when we find it, but we are looking for something bigger. Eros—romantic love—sweeps us off our feet for a time, but it does not last forever. What we want—in fact, what we were created to need—is someone who loves us unconditionally, with a love that looks out for us even when we do not deserve it. We need agape love.

My heart breaks for the countless millions who have a genuine, deep longing for love without any inkling of where they can find the type of love they need. Many of us believe that love is just a feeling. If we believe that, we will try to satisfy our deepest longing with the wrong type of love. When we don't get the love we need, we may blame our family ("My dad didn't love me enough") or our friends ("My friends don't make enough time for me") or our significant other ("The passion just isn't there anymore"). But the problem is not the people around us. The problem is that we are expecting something from them that they cannot give us.

We need to be loved unconditionally, and there is only one person who can love us like that. Jesus Christ. Jesus does not just love us because he feels like it. Jesus loves us because we need agape. He made us that way. Jesus is love, and he pours out his agape in a million different ways every day. He loves us so much that he provides for us in ways that we don't even acknowledge. His love is so great and so present that we often take it for granted.

THE SUN AND THE SON

Theologians sometimes talk about "common grace," which is a way of talking about the benefits everyone receives from God's goodness. Now we don't think about these very much or even ask him for them. For example, I have never asked God to make the sun rise in the morning. And to be honest, I rarely thank him for it. But that sun just keeps coming up every morning. That is part of God's common grace. There are certain things that God does for all of us just because he is good and because he loves us.

Jesus explained that common grace is so big that it even benefits the worst sinners in the world:

> You have heard that it was said, "Love your neighbor and hate your enemy." But I tell you, love your enemies and pray for those who persecute you, that you may be children of your Father in heaven. He causes his sun to rise on the evil and the good, and sends rain on the righteous and the unrighteous.
>
> MATTHEW 5:43–45

Jesus says that God causes "his sun" to rise on the evil and the good. It is not an accident that Jesus refers to the sun as God's sun. It is intentional. Jesus is saying that God created the sun, and therefore God owns the sun (along with everything else in the universe). And everybody benefits from the sun—rich and poor, atheist and believer, good and evil, sinner and saint. Common grace.

Sometimes we forget simple things. If God has the whole world in his hands, if he is in complete control, what are we so worried about? If he has the whole world in his hands, surely he can take care of us in the world. If his eye is on the sparrow, surely he is paying attention to us. He raised his sun this morning for you. He is working for you without your even asking for it. That is agape love. That is how Jesus loves.

I have a friend who works in financial services. He is always telling me about the market, about how one company is a good investment and another is going to plummet, about risks and returns, about how one of his stock picks was a great success or how he sold a stock because it was not performing as well as it should. Every time we talk, I think about two things. One, I'm glad I don't work in financial services. Two, I'm glad God doesn't get rid of me because of a poor performance. God continues to invest in me because he knows that one day the investment will pay off. One day I will be everything that God made me to be. My stock might be down today, but one day it is going to skyrocket.

I love that Jesus refers to the sun as an example of how God loves people. I love it because there are striking similarities between God's sun and God's Son, Jesus Christ. The sun is amazing evidence of God's common grace, but God's greatest gift to the world was not the sun. It was his Son.

The sun helps to light the physical world, but the Son is

the spiritual light of the world. Both the sun and the Son have been worshiped, but only the Son has responded. Both are high and lifted up, but only the Son can draw all people to him. Both are an all-consuming fire, but only the Son can melt a cold heart. Both are so vast they cannot be comprehended, but only the Son is intimately acquainted with every detail of our lives. Both witnessed the birth of humanity, but it was the Son that God used to create humanity. Both sustain life, but only the Son gives everlasting life. Both are enthroned in the heavens, but only the Son is King of kings and Lord of lords. Both rise to declare a new day, but only the Son rose to declare victory over death, hell, and the grave, and to give new life to humanity.

God did not have to make the sun rise this morning, and he did not have to give us his Son. But he did. Because he loves us. He did not have to raise the widow's son from the dead. But he did. Because he loves. Oh, how he loves!

Chapter Six

GET UP

*Then he went up and touched the bier they were carrying
him on, and the bearers stood still. He said, "Young
man, I say to you, get up!" The dead man sat up and
began to talk, and Jesus gave him back to his mother.
They were all filled with awe and praised God. "A great
prophet has appeared among us," they said. "God has
come to help his people." This news about Jesus spread
throughout Judea and the surrounding country.*

LUKE 7:14–17

LOVE LETTERS

Is anything more awkward than young love? I'm talking *young*
love, like elementary school love. Remember how you liked
that girl with the pigtails and the big smile or that boy with
the big buck teeth? Remember love notes? That is typically
how young love happened. Without the notes there would
have been little "romantic" communication between boys and
girls. Love notes had a structure and served a purpose. If you
had a crush on someone, you did not just walk up and say
that. That would be madness, not to mention way too easy
and clear. Instead, you wrote (in your best cursive) a note to
your crush, maybe drew a heart or two, and then got your best
friend to deliver the note. If your friend put in a good word or
two for you, all the better.

The notes I sent were all similar, a series of questions with
multiple choice answers and escalating commitment. I left no
room for error and not much room for mystery.

- Do you like me? Please circle one.
  Yes. No. Maybe.
- Do you love me? Please circle one.
  Yes. No. Maybe.
- Do you want to be my girlfriend? Please circle one.
  Yes. No. Maybe.

On one occasion I sent a note to a girl and she circled "No," then another "No," and then "Maybe." I guess she was confused. She clearly did not like me or love me, but she was considering being my girlfriend. Weird. If I received a note I was a perpetual "Maybe" circler. I did not want to have a girlfriend most of the time, but I also did not want to break girls' hearts. Hey, don't hate the player, hate the game.

Once you get past about seventh grade, however, you realize that real love does not work this way. If you love someone you have to go to them in person. You can't hide behind your best friend or a little note.

When I met my wife, she made me work for it. For the first few months after we met, I called her frequently, but she never returned my calls, not even once. You would think that I would have gotten the hint, but I'm not that quick. And DawnCheré is that beautiful, so I persisted. When it came to DawnCheré, I didn't want to leave things up to a little love note with multiple choice answers. I wanted her to know *me*, not my grammar.

I am always amazed when I meet believers who focus so strongly on right behavior that it seems like they love God's Law more than they love the Lawgiver. Why would you worship God's love letters when you can worship God himself? Sure, God gave us the Law (through Moses), but he also gave us Jesus, the embodiment of grace and truth. Grace is a person. Truth is a person. His name is Jesus, and he had no problem pursuing you personally. Jesus came from heaven to make a way to be with you. He initiated it. He first loved you, before you could love him. He desired a person-to-person relationship, not a distant wave, not a side-hug, not an exchange of elementary love letters. He wanted a loving, intimate, personal relationship with us. And here is something amazing: Once you experience a relationship with God, you will find yourself *wanting* to do all those things you used to think you *had* to do in order to earn God's love.

The Full Extent of His Love

In John 13, we read that just before Jesus was arrested and crucified he took the time to eat a meal with his disciples and to teach them one more lesson. During the meal Jesus poured water into a basin, walked around the room, and washed the disciples' feet. This was an incredible display of humility. Here was Jesus, the most famous rabbi of his day and the teacher and mentor of this group of men. They had left their previous interests and jobs behind to follow him. They believed that he was the Messiah, the long-awaited Savior of Israel. They revered Jesus. And yet Jesus bent down in front of each of them and played the role of a servant. He washed their filthy, mud-caked feet and explained that they were to serve one another as he had served them.

John explains that this lesson helped show the disciples the full extent of Jesus' love for them. He would serve them as they needed to be served. There was no length to which Jesus would not go to love them. Jesus pursued the disciples, and he demonstrated his love not only by washing their feet but also by dying on the cross. In other words, Jesus loved them right to the end. True love never quits pursuing, even to the end.

Nine years ago I married DawnCheré, but just because we're married doesn't mean I have stopped pursuing her. The marriage vows we made were not just for the honeymoon week or the first year or until we tired of each other. Our commitment is for life. So for the rest of my life I will chase her. I will pursue her. It is pursuing that produces the passion.

When a couple is dating, the pursuit is intense. He doesn't stop calling her. She can't stop thinking about him. The warm fuzzies are everywhere. Often, though, when the couple gets married, they stop dating each other and the pursuit goes cold. The relationship goes stale. DawnCheré and I have committed not to allow ourselves to settle for a marriage built on good times gone by. We want our love to grow deeper with time. That means we have to keep pursuing each other.

When it comes to our relationship with Jesus, even after he saves us he doesn't stop pursuing us. Philippians 1:6 says that "he who began a good work in you will carry it on to completion until the day of Christ Jesus." In other words, Jesus isn't a player. He doesn't save you only to drop you and then go "get" someone else. Jesus is in it with you for the long haul. He is making you into something. You are his masterpiece, and he isn't going to settle until everything is just right.

The Bible is full of verses proclaiming God's persistent love. Here are several:

> The steadfast love of the LORD never ceases;
> his mercies never come to an end;

they are new every morning;
great is your faithfulness.

LAMENTATIONS 3:22–23 ESV

Give thanks to the LORD, for he is good.
His love endures forever.
Give thanks to the God of gods.
His love endures forever.
Give thanks to the Lord of lords:
His love endures forever.

PSALM 136:1–3

God's law was given so that all people could see how sinful they were. But as people sinned more and more, God's
wonderful grace became more abundant.

ROMANS 5:20 NLT

Love knows no limit to its endurance, no end to its trust,
no fading of its hope; it can outlast anything. It is, in fact, the
one thing that still stands when all else has fallen.

1 CORINTHIANS 13:7–8 PHILLIPS

I could go on for pages. If you are interested in more of
this, there is a fantastic book called the Bible, which will reveal
much more to you about how much love is behind God's pursuit of you. Check it out.

Jesus loves us. His love knows no limits. Therefore, Jesus
pursues us. He cannot stop loving and therefore will not stop
pursuing until the Last Day. In the widow's story we see the

pursuit up close and personal, and we catch a glimpse of the unfathomable love that Jesus has for us.

HE TOUCHED THE STRETCHER

Jesus saw the widow walking in the funeral procession and he approached her. Interestingly, the text says nothing about the woman's faith or lack of it. Maybe she was a faith-filled woman of God. Maybe not. Maybe she was still so down from the loss of her husband, and then the loss of her son, that her faith in God had dwindled. Maybe she doubted that God existed. Maybe she never had faith in God. We don't know. Luke doesn't mention it. I think this was intentional.

Whatever the case may have been, like the centurion in the earlier story, the widow could never have deserved what Jesus was about to do for her. She could have been the holiest woman in Nain, and still she could not have deserved the mighty love and grace of God. But God's love for us is not dependent on our love for him. We don't know the state of the widow's heart. What we do know is that when Jesus saw the widow mourning over the death of her son, his heart broke for her and he was compelled to act.

Jesus walked over to the bier and touched it. "Then he went up and touched the bier they were carrying him on, and the bearers stood still."

Now, before we go any further, we need to understand that under the Jewish law, interacting with dead bodies was strictly forbidden. If a person touched a corpse, he was considered "unclean" for an entire week: "Whoever touches a human corpse will be unclean for seven days" (Numbers 19:11).

When Jesus touched the stretcher and the men carrying it stood still, I'm guessing they were shocked. "What is Rabbi Jesus doing?" they must have thought. They knew that touching a dead person would make Jesus unclean. So what was the point?

I think that in this moment Jesus was (as usual) teaching something about God and the gospel. Jesus was showing that no power—not sickness, not grief, not people's expectations, not even death—can separate us from his love. He wasn't afraid of walking right into the middle of a mess to demonstrate his love. He went right to the edge of uncleanliness in order to love this widow and her son. In fact, that is largely what the gospel is all about: a divine Savior who chose to walk among humanity, not to make bad people good, but to make dead people alive.

What a picture! The message of the gospel is that when we could not get to God, he came to us. Jesus initiated. He pursued. He did not care what it looked like to everyone else. He knew the risks, and he knew they were worth it.

Many people make the story of Jesus all about morality. Jesus was a great moral teacher, they say, and he taught many wonderful things. Love your neighbor as yourself, forgive people when they hurt you, turn the other cheek. And they tell us that Jesus' life is an example worth following, like Gandhi or Martin Luther King Jr. If we can just be a little more like Jesus every day, they say, we will be better off. We should try to do more nice things and less bad things. It is like they think that Jesus came to earth to give us a little makeover.

But Jesus did not come to earth for a makeover. He came

for a takeover! He came to defeat sin once and for all. He came to conquer death, the consequence of sin. Sin doesn't just make you immoral. It's worse than that. Sin makes you dead. Spiritually, we are dead because of our sins, but God gives us new life through Jesus Christ (Ephesians 2:5). It is all well and good to try to live like Jesus. It's great to do nice things, and we are all better off when we try to be more like Jesus. But make no mistake, Jesus is more than just a great moral teacher or an example to follow. He is the King of kings and the Lord of lords. He is our Savior. He is the Son of God. And when he reached down into humanity, it wasn't just to teach us how to live better lives. It was to rescue us from the things that have plagued humanity since the Garden of Eden incident: sin and death.

The dead young man in the story, lifeless and therefore helpless, is a picture of humanity apart from Jesus. We all fall short of God's standard because we all have sinned. And our sin has left us spiritually lifeless and helpless. Do you know what a dead man can do to make himself alive? Nothing. He's dead. In our sin we are utterly unable to make ourselves alive. To accomplish that we need God's intervention. So Jesus stops the funeral procession and walks straight to the young man. What a beautiful hint of what was to come, for the son, for the widow, and for us.

Later, when Jesus went to the cross he went far beyond just getting next to death. He took on death itself. He would not simply test the limits of ceremonial cleanliness. He would *become* sin and also defeat death so that we might be given new life and be called the sons and daughters of God. Only an author gets to rewrite his story. Only God gets to throw away death. And he did. Jesus pursued us when we had nothing to offer in return. In our sin and shame Jesus died for us. Romans 5:7–8 tells us: "Very rarely will anyone die for a righteous person, though for a good person someone might possibly dare to die. But God demonstrates his own love for us in this: While we were still sinners, Christ died for us."

Jesus is not afraid of a mess. He is not intimidated by the dark and dead areas within you. In fact, you could say that he is the Messiah of the mess because the mess is where he does his best work. As we are about to see, Jesus is in the business of resurrecting, redeeming, and restoring. And if he can do it for one, he can do it for everyone.

GET UP

When Jesus touches the stretcher, the crowd stands still. There is silence, except for a few sniffles and sobs. The funeral attendees are confused. Even the disciples are not sure what is coming. All eyes are on Jesus. Finally, he speaks.

> "Young man, I say to you, get up!" The dead man sat up and
> began to talk, and Jesus gave him back to his mother.
>
> LUKE 7:14–15

Um, what? Jesus told a dead man to get up, and he got up, and he did not even touch the guy? No CPR? No mouth-to-mouth? No defibrillator? None of that. Just a word from the Son of God. Remember the centurion and how Jesus just spoke a word and healed the centurion's servant? Are you seeing a pattern here? When Jesus speaks, it's kind of a big deal.

Jesus crashes into this dead guy's life—actually his death—and basically says, "The funeral has been cancelled." That's a statement every Jesus follower should keep in mind every step of the way. We deserved death. We were dead in our sins. But Jesus came and declared, "The funeral has been cancelled!"

Jesus tells the young man to get up and the man sits up and speaks. We have no idea what he said. Maybe it was, "Man, that was a great nap!" or, "I just had the craziest dream!" or maybe just a simple, "Hey." Whatever it was, the crowd must have been dumbfounded. This kid was about to be buried. Now he is sitting up and talking.

In my mind the scene unfolds like one of those movies where someone does something heroic, but everyone is shocked that it happened, so no one says anything for a second. They're dazed. They're staring at the hero. It's silent. Then one person starts to clap. Then another person starts clapping. Then another. And before long the whole crowd erupts into cheers and applause.

I love how Eugene Peterson describes this scene in *The Message*:

> When Jesus saw her, his heart broke. He said to her, "Don't cry." Then he went over and touched the coffin. The pallbearers stopped. He said, "Young man, I tell you: Get up." The dead son sat up and began talking. Jesus presented him to his mother.
>
> They all realized they were in a place of holy mystery,

that God was at work among them. They were quietly worshipful—and then noisily grateful, calling out among themselves, "God is back, looking to the needs of his people!" The news of Jesus spread all through the country.

LUKE 7:15–17

"Quietly worshipful—and then noisily grateful." It's the holy slow-clap! Our own response to Jesus today should look something like this, quiet worship leading to noisy gratitude. His love changes us from the inside out. He raises us from death to life. He melts stone cold hearts. He literally makes us new persons in Christ. That's a thought that should leave us awestruck and make our jaws drop. We should meditate on it night and day in quiet, reverent worship of the God of such amazing grace and glory.

But we should not stop there. Our quiet worship should turn into noisy gratitude. We were dead, but now we are alive! Let's not continue acting as if we are dead! Our quiet worship ought to compel us to proclaim the name of Jesus, our Savior, as loud as we can. Notice that when the young man comes back to life, everyone worships God. Why? Because a life resurrected by God always points people to God.

"Get up." How much meaning is packed into that little sentence? When Jesus spoke these words to a dead man, he had no choice but to come back to life. When Jesus pursues us, he gets us, even when we are dead. This young man had no choice in the matter. The God of the universe had commanded his creation to come back to life, and it did. When Jesus crashes into our lives, we wake up. But notice that this is not just about being awake. Jesus' words were, "Get up." Now that he's awake, the young man has a choice. He can lie there on the stretcher or obey Jesus and get up and get going.

After Jesus wakes us up spiritually, we are given a choice: continue to live in sin as we always have or get up and obey Jesus' call. This is the Christian life. Everything we do is in response to what Jesus has already done. All of our godly behavior is rooted in our thanks to the Savior. For example, we don't love one another because we have to. We love one another because Jesus loved us first, and this is how we thank him. We don't witness to other people just because Jesus commanded us to do it. We witness because we can't help it. We witness because we have seen Jesus do something amazing in our lives and we can't help but talk about it. We don't give because of some obligation to give. We give because we have been given more than we could ever give away. We don't serve to earn God's favor. We serve because it is an honor to resemble the one who first served us. Our worship, our sacrifice, our discipline, and our perseverance is our reasonable response to the amazing grace of Jesus Christ.

"Get up." Will you? Or will you stay down, like so many people choose to do? Even after encountering Jesus and being transformed from death to life, many believers allow their pain and sorrow to control them. They let their setbacks and mistakes define them. They put their faith in the same people who let them down before. In other words, they keep on building the same old sandcastles.

My friend, Jesus wants to set you free, but you have to be willing to walk out of the prison. It is time to get up, move on, and build your life upon something new, something strong, something that will last forever. It is time to get going.

I love how the psalmist David puts it:

> *I waited patiently for the LORD;*
> *he turned to me and heard my cry.*
> *He lifted me out of the slimy pit,*
> *out of the mud and mire;*
> *he set my feet on a rock*
> *and gave me a firm place to stand.*
> *He put a new song in my mouth,*
> *a hymn of praise to our God.*
> *Many will see and fear the LORD*
> *and put their trust in him.*

PSALM 40:1–3

In this psalm David says that God lifted him out of a "slimy pit, out of the mud and mire." Life feels like that sometimes, doesn't it? Like we're stuck in a dark, stinking, slippery, slimy pit. Like there is no way out. But David says that God pulled him out of the pit and set his feet on a rock, a firm foundation, a solid place to stand. No more slime. No more mud. No more shaky ground. And in that moment David sings a new song of praise about God's redeeming love.

HAPPY TREES

Life is going to happen. We people are fragile. Jesus doesn't promise us a problem-free life, but he does promise that no matter what we face he will walk through it with us, even though we never know where the next step might lead. When I was growing up my mom always said, "Don't give up today. Tomorrow is on the way." You never know what tomorrow holds.

When we were in middle school, my brother and I liked to watch one particular TV show about art. Now, my brother and I are fairly creative, but we are not art lovers. Neither of us can paint or sculpt or even appreciate those things, frankly. But this was no ordinary art. It was dramatic art.

The show was called *The Joy of Painting*, featuring the artist Bob Ross. He was an interesting-looking guy. He had a big afro (pretty impressive for a white dude—should we call it a whitefro?), and he usually wore half-buttoned shirts with denim bell-bottoms. Groovy. And the show was simple because Bob was teaching viewers how to paint as he did. He would start with a blank canvas and then spend thirty minutes painting a picture and explaining the steps as he went along, from the brushes and strokes he used to the colors, techniques, and inspiration for the scene. Usually he painted nature scenes with mountains, lakes, rivers, creeks, hills, and clouds. I know it doesn't sound like much, but Bob was the master of making art dramatic.

He had a way of lulling you into a kind of trance and inviting you into the painting. His voice was quiet, almost as if he was afraid he might scare the paint if he talked too loud. In almost a whisper he would instruct you about his painting, along the way continually saying things like: "Maybe a happy little rock lives right there. Let's put a cloud right here. Here's a happy little fella." Bob's voice was the most peaceful sound in the world.

My brother and I would watch from start to finish as Bob transformed a blank canvas into a majestic mountain range with a crystal clear lake in the foreground. He would color the sky like a sunset, and in our eyes the painting would then look complete. The scene was lovely, inspiring even. But the show wasn't quite over. Out of nowhere, Bob would say something like, "Hmm. Something is missing." And then without warning he would take black paint and make a giant squiggly mark right down the middle of the canvas! As soon as he did it we would start shouting at the TV.

"No! Don't do it! You're ruining it! Stop! Everything looked so nice!"

We just knew that all of Bob's beautiful work was going to go to waste. What was he doing? What was he thinking? A black line here, a dark smudge there. He was turning this masterpiece into a mess. It looked fine, but now he wrecking the whole thing.

But just when all seemed lost, Bob would say, "Let's put a happy little tree here, and some more over here." And so he would add more paint to the black streaks and turn them into trees. Before long there was a whole forest. Then he would brush some white paint on the edges of the dark smudges and magically turn them into bushes on the edge of the lake. When he finally finished, the painting was much more beautiful than we thought it was before the black marks and smudges. The trees and bushes and extra little touches added depth and character to the scene. They made it more real, more beautiful.

Bob took what looked like a terrible mess and turned it into one of the most beautiful pieces of art my brother and I had ever seen. We would look at each other and say, with relief, "Thank God he didn't listen to us."

Looking back, it was silly for us kids to doubt Bob Ross, the master painter. After all, what did we know about painting? Who made us experts on what the picture needed or did not need? What art had we ever created?

Following Jesus is a lot like watching Bob Ross paint. We may think our lives are great the way they are. We may be comfortable and think we have it all under control. We may even think that our lives are beautiful. And then out of nowhere a big black streak gets painted right across our lives, and we panic. "Where are you, Jesus? What are you doing? Why are you letting this happen? You're ruining my life!"

But if we just hang on a little longer, we see that God knew what he was doing all along. That black mark was no accident. God wasn't asleep at the wheel. He knew just what he was doing. And he did not leave us in our mess. God is into completing things, and when he does that he makes them beautiful.

Know this: where you are today is not necessarily where you will be tomorrow. Put your life in Jesus' hands and then watch him turn it into a masterpiece. That black mark running right down the middle of your life may well turn into the majestic tree that gives your entire life depth and beauty. Remember that things are not always as they appear. Even death itself is no match for our loving Savior. Your future may seem dead, but as we have seen with the widow's son, God is making dead things live.

The widow seemed to have lost everything. But the most amazing part of her story is that she encountered the solid rock on which to build her life, one that would stand strong through heartache, sorrow, and even death. Her son was raised to life, but he would eventually die again. But this time the widow's house would not be built on sand. It would be built on the Rock.

Part Three

THE PREACHER

John's disciples told him about all these things. Calling two
of them, he sent them to the Lord to ask, "Are you the one
who is to come, or should we expect someone else?"
When the men came to Jesus, they said, "John the
Baptist sent us to you to ask, 'Are you the one who is
to come, or should we expect someone else?'"
At that very time Jesus cured many who had diseases, sicknesses
and evil spirits, and gave sight to many who were blind. So he
replied to the messengers, "Go back and report to John what
you have seen and heard: The blind receive sight, the lame
walk, those who have leprosy are cleansed, the deaf hear, the
dead are raised, and the good news is proclaimed to the poor.
Blessed is anyone who does not stumble on account of me."
After John's messengers left, Jesus began to speak to the crowd
about John: "What did you go out into the wilderness to see?
A reed swayed by the wind? If not, what did you go out to see?
A man dressed in fine clothes? No, those who wear expensive

clothes and indulge in luxury are in palaces. But what did
you go out to see? A prophet? Yes, I tell you, and more than
a prophet. This is the one about whom it is written:

"'I will send my messenger ahead of you,
who will prepare your way before you.'

I tell you, among those born of women there is no
one greater than John; yet the one who is least in
the kingdom of God is greater than he."
(All the people, even the tax collectors, when they heard
Jesus' words, acknowledged that God's way was right,
because they had been baptized by John. But the Pharisees
and the experts in the law rejected God's purpose for
themselves, because they had not been baptized by John.)
Jesus went on to say, "To what, then, can I compare the people
of this generation? What are they like? They are like children
sitting in the marketplace and calling out to each other:

'We played the pipe for you,
and you did not dance;
we sang a dirge,
and you did not cry.'

For John the Baptist came neither eating bread nor drinking
wine, and you say, 'He has a demon.' The Son of Man
came eating and drinking, and you say, 'Here is a glutton
and a drunkard, a friend of tax collectors and sinners.'
But wisdom is proved right by all her children."

LUKE 7:18–35

Chapter Seven

JOHN THE DOUBTER

*John's disciples told him about all these things. Calling two
of them, he sent them to the Lord to ask, "Are you the one
who is to come, or should we expect someone else?"*

Luke 7:18–19

Drowning

When I moved back to Miami from Cleveland, Tennessee, after college I needed a hobby and I thought diving would fit the bill. One of my favorite things about Miami is the water. The city is right on the edge of the mighty Atlantic Ocean, home to some of the best scuba diving spots in the world. As a teenager I always enjoyed snorkeling. It is so peaceful floating on top of the water, staring down at the beautiful coral reefs. What can I say? Sea life has always intrigued me, probably because of my deep-seated love of *The Little Mermaid*—the movie, not the mermaid. Seriously, "Part of Your World," a song from the soundtrack, is a Top Ten all-time song. (I don't care what you say. Haters gonna hate.) I didn't have gills or fins so I figured scuba diving was the next best thing.

Getting a scuba license is not hard, but there is a process to it. First you have to get the gear. And honestly, that is my favorite part of any sport's activity. My house is littered with the gear of hobbies gone by—cycling, hunting, basketball. It's never just about how well you perform. It's about how you look while you do it, and I was going to look good—at least as good as a man can look in a wetsuit and a diving mask. I made sure all my gadgets were the sleekest and coolest. If Apple had made a scuba pressure gauge, I would have bought it. (The iGauge—you're welcome, Apple.)

Once you have bought all the gear and figured out how to dress the part, half the battle has been won. Then comes the hard part, actually learning the sport. In scuba diving, there is some initial testing involved. The first part is a written exam. You read a book and answer questions based on it. Cake.

But the real question is whether you can apply the information, so for the second part of the test you go underwater, but in a controlled environment, a swimming pool. That's where you learned the fundamentals, such as how to assemble the equipment, how to clear the mask, how to equalize your ears.

After a few lessons in the pool, my time for the real thing had arrived. The ocean. Our class had to complete two separate dives in order to get licensed. We started on the beach and swam to the reef where the dive would take place. The first dive we did went perfectly.

The second dive was a different story. There were about fifteen of us in the class. We began swimming out to the reef and were about forty yards from shore when we spotted a swimmer bobbing up and down. He was panicking and crying out for help, arms flailing back and forth, head in and out of the water. Without hesitation, our instructor made a beeline straight for the man. I have never seen anyone swim so fast. Dude was like Aquaman.

When our instructor got to the drowning man and reached out to help him, the man pushed him away. That happened again, and by now the swimmer's face was barely above the water. One more time our instructor grabbed the

man, and this time the man grabbed back. In fact, he grabbed
our instructor and began pulling him under the water. We all
watched in terror, not knowing what to do. The swimmer was
doing whatever he could to stay above water, but in the process
he was dunking the person who was trying to save him.

Finally, somehow, the instructor got control. He shouted,
"Quit panicking or you will drown the both of us!" By the
grace of God the swimmer calmed down and my instructor
got him back to the shore.

I remember thinking about this event much later and feeling like God spoke to me through it: "Rich, this is what so
many of my people look like." Without Jesus we are all drowning, and when you're drowning, you need someone to save you.
You don't need someone to toss you a book on how to swim.
It's too late, then, for a how-to book. If you don't know how to
swim and you are drowning, you need someone to rescue you.
You need the Savior.

Many of us know that Jesus came to rescue us, but for
some reason, instead of letting him do that work, we panic and
do everything we can to save ourselves. We forget that we don't
know how to swim. The truth is, there is nothing we can do to
save ourselves. Either we let Jesus save us or we drown.

One way people try to save themselves is through what
is commonly known as "religion." What do you think about
when you hear that word? Christianity? Islam? Judaism?
Prayers? Holy books? Priests? Robes? Maybe the word *religion*
stirs up good thoughts in your head. Maybe not. Maybe you
have been burned by a religion, or maybe you think every religious person is crazy. It is hard to define what religion means

because the word means different things to different people. Here is what I mean when I use that word: religion is belief and behavior based on man's conception of God.

Religion can be a good thing. If a person believes that God exists, it makes sense that his understanding of life and his behavior should be shaped by his understanding of God. And in many cases that can be a good thing. But like the other sandcastles we have looked at, sometimes religion doesn't hold up under the weight of life. It can be like a "How to Swim" manual—full of helpful truths and tips. But if you're drowning and can't swim, it is not very helpful.

Also, religion says, "If I obey all of God's rules, God will look out for me." So we try to obey. We try really hard. And sometimes we do a really good job. But ultimately, religion does not make us proud of God. It makes us proud of ourselves. And then somewhere on the journey we begin to believe that we can be good enough for God. We convince ourselves that rule keeping and ritual obedience will keep us out of harm's way.

At some point, most of us are tempted to build a life on religion. Once we start believing things about God, we are tempted to place more importance in our beliefs than in our God. Even the best of us can fall victim to this snare. This one tempted even the most devoted of Jesus' followers.

John the Baptist

The third story of our four stories in Luke 7 is one of the most fascinating in the Bible. Like the previous two stories, it tells us about a person experiencing a very low point and almost without hope. Then Jesus shows up and does the unexpected. But unlike the other two stories, this one is about a person we are familiar with. It is not an unnamed Roman centurion or an unknown Jewish widow. And for Jesus himself, this person was family. Luke 7:18–35 is about John the Baptist. You may have a favorite Bible character. John the Baptist is at the top of my list (excluding Jesus, of course—calm down).

John and Jesus were cousins. Can you imagine if you had had Jesus as your cousin when you were growing up? You wouldn't have had to worry about anything! You would have just walked around doing whatever you wanted, and if anyone got in your way, you would just say, "You have a problem? You want me to call Jesus? You saw what he did to that fig tree, didn't you?" (Now that I think about it, it's probably best that Jesus wasn't my cousin when I was growing up.)

John was a child of promise and purpose. You might recall from Luke 1 the story of his miraculous beginning. His father was a Jewish priest named Zechariah. We don't know how old Zechariah was, but the Bible says he was "very old." Zechariah and his wife, Elizabeth, had no children, but not because they lived the high life in a condo on the Mediterranean. Elizabeth had been unable to conceive.

One day, Zechariah was inside the temple doing his priest thing when an angel appeared to him. It scared Zechariah to death. (In the Bible, angels are way scary. Check it out for yourself.) The angel told Zechariah not to be afraid, and he said that Zechariah and Elizabeth would have a son and that they were to name him John. The angel said John would be a "joy and delight" to his parents and that many people would "rejoice because of his birth," because John would "be great in the sight of the Lord." The angel also said that John was to be set apart and even filled with the Holy Spirit before he was born. Most importantly, the angel said that John would call the people of Israel to repentance in order to make them ready for the appearance of the Messiah. So John was going to be a big deal.

Instead of thanking God or high-fiving the angel, or even smiling, Zechariah asks, "How can I be sure of this?" In other words, while he's staring at an angel of God Almighty, homeboy says, "Yeah right, angel. Prove it." So the angel tells Zechariah that because he doubted, he won't be able to speak a word until John is born. So poor, mute Zechariah walks out of the temple super excited but he can't say a word. The Bible says he was trying to act out what he had seen and heard, but the people could not understand him. That must have been the most frustrating game of charades ever!

Well, time goes by, and wouldn't you know it, Elizabeth becomes pregnant just like the angel said she would. A few months into that pregnancy, Mary, pregnant with Jesus, visits Elizabeth. The Bible says that when Elizabeth heard Mary's voice, John "leaped in her womb," and Elizabeth was filled with the Holy Spirit and she shouted, "Blessed are you among women, and blessed is the child you will bear!" Pretty cool. John the Baptist praised Jesus while they were both still in the womb.

After John was born, his zeal for God increased. He was devoted and very disciplined. He wasn't into pleasing people, only God. He moved out into the desert and started preaching. Forget that whole "have a beautiful temple and flashy website" thing. He had something much better: a word from the Lord. People came from all over to hear this guy preach. And not only did they listen, they responded with repentance and baptism.

Nothing about John was normal. Actually, "abnormal" is putting it lightly. John lived in the desert and wore clothes made from camel hair (itchy much?) with a leather belt strapped around his waist. And when it came to his diet, John was sort of a paleo guy: plenty of locusts and wild honey. Delish! Low on carbs, though, so he was probably pretty trim. Talk about a wild man!

John wasn't worried about impressing anyone, and he was never afraid of offending the "in crowd." Being marketed by man does not matter much when you have been marked by God. John spoke with such passion and authority that he made the people in power nervous. One time, he called the Pharisees and Sadducees, who had come to hear him preach, a "brood of vipers." In other words, he called them a group of slithering snakes. Not a great way to make friends. But John wasn't in it to make friends. He was simply obeying the call of God on his life, boldly and faithfully.

John's purpose was clear to him. He was the forerunner to the Messiah. This was a huge deal. In the Old Testament, God spoke through the prophet Malachi that he would send the prophet Elijah (long dead) before the day of the Lord came. Jewish rabbis often debated the meaning of this prophecy, so when John burst onto the scene preaching repentance and turning to God, the rabbis were intrigued. They knew what Malachi 4:6 promised about Elijah: "He will turn the hearts of the parents to their children, and the hearts of the children to their parents." Little did the rabbis knows that the angel had spoken similar words about John:

> He will bring back many of the people of Israel to the Lord their God. And he will go on before the Lord, in the spirit and power of Elijah, to turn the hearts of the parents to their children and the disobedient to the wisdom of the righteous—to make ready a people prepared for the Lord.
>
> LUKE 1:16–17

Could John be the promised Elijah? The rabbis wondered. When they interrogated the Baptist about who he was, he told them that he was not the Messiah. He simply said, "I am the voice of one calling in the wilderness, 'Make straight the way for the Lord'" (John 1:23).

John the Baptist's message was simple, and the crowds gathering around him grew. He was calling people to repentance and they were listening. As a sign of the change in their hearts, John said they needed to be baptized in water. And they did that. The ministry was booming. John was leading and his disciples were developing.

One day as John the Baptist was ministering, he saw Jesus and immediately shouted, "Look, the Lamb of God, who takes away the sin of the world!" (John 1:29). But Jesus was not coming to John to be worshiped that day. He was coming to be baptized. John, believing that Jesus was the Messiah, the

Savior of the world, tried to get out of it. Wouldn't you? Jesus was sinless. Why would he need to be baptized? John told Jesus that Jesus should be baptizing *him*. But Jesus insisted, so John obeyed.

When Jesus came up out of the water after being baptized, something amazing occurred. The heavens opened up and the Holy Spirit descended on Jesus in the form of a dove. Then a voice from heaven declared, "This is my Son, whom I love; with him I am well pleased" (Matthew 3:17). I have no idea what God's audible voice sounds like. I imagine it is like Mufasa from the *Lion King*. However it sounded, this was a confirmation moment. For the people at Jesus' baptism, there was now no denying who Jesus was. He was the Son of God. John knew this. That's why, sometime later, when Jesus' ministry was growing and people asked John about this, he said that Jesus "must become greater; I must become less" (John 3:30). John knew.

JOHN THE DOUBTER

The John the Baptist I learned about in Sunday school was strong, confident, bold, determined, fearless, and faithful. He was a prophet. He lived in the wilderness and wore clothes made out of camel hair, and he ate locusts, for crying out loud! But in Luke 7, we see a different side of John. Instead of John the Baptist, hero of the faith, we meet John the Doubter.

In Luke 7, John languishes in prison, having been sent there because he told the truth. That was John's thing, remember? Happy truth or hard truth, prophets just speak the truth. Sometimes people don't like to hear the truth, especially when the truth exposes a political leader who is having an affair with his sister-in-law, breaking up her marriage, and then marrying her. Can you say "scandal"? You didn't know this stuff was in the Bible, did you? Be honest.

Back in John's day there was a king named Herod who was the son of the Herod who tried to have Jesus killed when Jesus was a baby. The younger Herod, known as Herod Antipas, had married his own niece, Herodias, who happened to have been his own brother's wife. Nice family.

John the Baptist knew all about these reality TV relationships, and he told the truth about them. And to Herod personally, John said, "It is not lawful for you to have her" (Matthew 14:4). Herod got furious and wanted to kill John, but he was afraid because the people considered John a prophet. So he had John arrested and thrown into prison.

Now things get even crazier. While John is in prison, Herod's birthday rolls around. At his birthday party, Herodias's daughter (Herod's stepdaughter) dances for all of the guests. We don't know what kind of dance it was, but it must have been something. The Bible tells us that it pleased Herod so much that he promised to give her anything she wanted, up to half of his entire kingdom. In case you aren't paying attention: Herod's stepdaughter dances for him and his boys at his birthday party, and he gets so hot and bothered that he says he will give her up to half of everything he owns. (Someone call Child Protective Services!) She then runs to mom to ask what she should ask for. Her mom knows exactly what: the head of John the Baptist on a platter. So she makes that request to Herod and it's a done deal (see Matthew 14:6–11).

So that incestuously danced, birthday blowout bash and beheading party is on the horizon as John lies languishing in prison. There, he starts wondering. Here he is, a prophet of God Almighty, a beacon of truth, a faithful servant of God, and the man who paved the way for the Messiah to show up. John knew that his job was to announce that the Messiah was on the way and then that the Messiah was now here—the "Lamb of God, who takes away the sin of the world!" (John 1:29). So Jesus the Messiah had arrived and was demonstrating supernatural power. But John, languishing in one of those horrific Roman prisons, begins to have serious doubts about Jesus being the Messiah.

Circumstances can have a way of making us forget what we know is true. But let's not judge John too harshly. It is often hard to know what we really believe until a crisis comes. If you have never doubted your beliefs, it is probably because you have not experienced much hardship.

In my church, when we are considering a person for a leadership position, we like to know whether a person has been through tough times in his or her life—the death of a loved one, financial difficulty, sickness, or other such things. We want to know this not because we are fond of a good sob story, but because it is hard to know whether a person really believes something unless he or she has held onto his or her belief through tough times.

If you have never been tested, can you really be trusted? People who tell me they have never doubted their faith typically are people who have never been in a serious battle. They've never been cut, never been bruised. When people get knocked down enough, it makes them wonder whether all that they thought they knew about God's loving them and being for them is actually true.

Consider two of Jesus' own disciples. Peter was absolutely certain of his devotion to Jesus, telling Jesus that he would follow him anywhere, even if that meant dying for him. But when Jesus was arrested and it became clear to Peter that Jesus was on his way to be crucified, Peter got scared. He was so scared, in fact, that when a little girl asked Peter if he were one of Jesus' disciples, Peter denied even knowing Jesus.

And what about Thomas? I feel sorry for Thomas. This poor guy's name is now synonymous with words like *uncertainty*, *skepticism*, and *indecision*. And, of course, he is one of the few disciples who still has a nickname two thousand years later, "Doubting Thomas."

After Jesus died and was resurrected, all the disciples gathered together for a reunion with Jesus. All of them had seen the risen Jesus already, except Thomas. When the disciples explained to Thomas that Jesus was alive, he didn't believe them. Would you? Thomas knew that Jesus had died. How could someone dead be alive? Thomas told them, "Unless I see the nail marks in his hands and put my finger where the nails were, and put my hand into his side, I will not believe" (John 20:25). Thomas's belief was being tested, big time, and he doubted.

Make no mistake. We all get tempted by doubt, even people closest to Jesus. John may even have wondered, "Where is Jesus? Surely he wouldn't just leave me here. Why hasn't he busted me out of jail? Why is he taking so long? Maybe he doesn't know I'm here. Maybe he isn't even the true Messiah."

It is easy to believe that Jesus is "for you" when things are going well, but when things are not so great, doubt can set in. And we wonder.

If Jesus is good, why does bad stuff keep happening to me?

If Jesus loves me, why did my dad leave me?

If Jesus loves me, why did I lose my job?

If Jesus is all-powerful, why was I abused?

Many of us sit in our own prison cells and wonder the same thing John wondered: Is Jesus really who I thought he was?

GO ASK HIM

Finally, John the Baptist couldn't take it anymore. He had been sitting in prison for so long that he had to know if Jesus was really the true Messiah. So he called for two of his disciples and told them to ask Jesus a simple question: "Are you the one who is to come, or should we expect someone else?" (Luke 7:19). In other words, "Jesus, are you the true Messiah or not?" John's disciples must have been dumbfounded when John said this. I bet they protested.

"What do you mean 'Go ask Jesus if he's the Messiah'? Seriously, John? We've been following you around in the hot desert sun eating bugs while you preached about the Messiah. And now you're doubting the whole thing?"

"John, don't you remember when you first saw Jesus and you said you were unfit to untie his sandals? Don't you remember saying that Jesus would baptize with the Holy Spirit and with fire? Don't you remember that when you baptized Jesus the heavens opened and God himself said that Jesus was his Son? And now you want us to go ask Jesus who he is? This is so embarrassing!"

I imagine John looking at these two guys and saying, "I know, fellas, but I'm in here and you're out there."

It is easy to believe when you are free of serious troubles, but when you are trapped and there is no hope in sight, doubt can set in, along with all of its disturbing questions.

QUESTIONS

I have learned that questions don't scare God, but they sure can rule over us. Sometimes it only takes one little question to make a person's faith crumble like sand. I think Satan knows this and uses it to his advantage. He has been doing it since the Garden of Eden, as we learn in Genesis 3:1–7.

God created the world, and he made it good. He made a beautiful garden and put a man (Adam) and a woman (Eve) in it. It was paradise on earth. The man and the woman were tasked with subduing the earth and exercising dominion over it. They had full reign over God's creation. There was just one rule: Don't eat from the tree in the middle of the garden.

One day, as Eve was walking past that particular tree, the serpent spoke to her, tempting her to eat from that tree. In the ensuing conversation between Eve and the serpent, I can imagine Eve beginning to question God's plan: "It's hard to remember exactly what God said about that tree. We talk all the time. Maybe he didn't say we could *never* eat from it. Maybe he was just waiting until we were ready to eat from it. Maybe he meant that there were certain times we shouldn't eat from it. I wonder what it tastes like. I bet it's really good, just like everything else God made. Is God keeping something from us? Does he really want what's best for us, or is he keeping the best for himself? Surely a little taste wouldn't hurt."

You know the rest of the story. And centuries have passed, but Satan still uses this tactic. He tempts us to question things we already know are true. And when circumstances are at the worst, when the questions are often the hardest to answer, the questions can turn into doubts.

John the Baptist had been so certain about who Jesus was, but his grievous circumstances made him question that certainty. It wasn't that he stopped believing. He just was not as certain as he had been. There is a big difference between doubt and unbelief. Unbelief is the opposite of faith. Doubt is not unbelief. In his book *Doubt and Assurance,* R. C. Sproul writes about this important distinction: "An all-important difference exists, therefore, between the open-minded uncertainty of doubt and the closed-minded certainty of unbelief." Doubt remains open to God's guidance and teaching. Unbelief has made up its mind against God. John doubted. And I can relate. But here's the thing. Jesus did not leave John alone with his doubts. He responded to them.

Chapter Eight

BE BLESSED

*When the men came to Jesus, they said, "John the
Baptist sent us to you to ask, 'Are you the one who
is to come, or should we expect someone else?'"*
*At that very time Jesus cured many who had diseases, sicknesses
and evil spirits, and gave sight to many who were blind. So he
replied to the messengers, "Go back and report to John what
you have seen and heard: The blind receive sight, the lame
walk, those who have leprosy are cleansed, the deaf hear, the
dead are raised, and the good news is proclaimed to the poor.
Blessed is anyone who does not stumble on account of me."*

LUKE 7:20–23

God Is Not a Copilot

I'm a control freak. I hate feeling like a situation is out of my hands. It doesn't matter what the situation is. I panic a little if I'm not controlling it. My wife knows this, and it is why I always drive the car. This is not up for discussion. If DawnCheré and I are driving somewhere, I'm in the driver's seat. Why? Because I have a future and a hope, and I don't want her messing that up! If we're going to crash, I want to be behind the wheel when we do. I love my wife, but I'm not willing to bet my life on her driving skills. (By the way, it would be great for me if you wouldn't mention this to her.)

I've said that I have to fly a lot. I've flown over two million miles on American Airlines alone, and that number climbs every year. Even so, I'm still not totally comfortable with the flying. I'm not a pilot. I know almost nothing about flying airplanes. I do know that if there is a problem while we're in the air, we can't just pull over and let the pilot have a look at the engine. If there is a problem, there is thirty thousand feet of thin air between us and safety. So every time I step onto a plane, I realize that my life depends on the pilot. This is difficult for me.

I start wondering: "Who is this guy? How long has he been flying? Did he sleep well last night? Did he sleep *at all*

137

last night? Does he have a family? Does he love his family? Is he going through any sort of emotional distress that I ought to know about?" When I saw *Flight*, a Denzel Washington movie about a pilot who drinks on the job, I panicked. "What if I have one of *those* pilots?" But they don't give passengers that information. They just tell you when to board, and you trust that everything will be fine. Most of the time you don't even get to meet the pilot, let alone interview him about his flight experience and mental health. I find that challenging.

Now, even though I find it hard not to worry about the pilot, I have noticed that whenever the plane passes through turbulence I never jump out of my seat and demand to speak with the pilot. And I never consider jumping out of the plane. I sit in my seat, listen to the pilot's instructions, and do whatever he says. Because he is the pilot; I am not.

I remember during one flight with some particularly rough turbulence, the pilot said, "In order to find smoother air we're going to have to climb to a higher altitude." I thought, "Oh snap! This pilot is preaching to us!" In life we all go through periods of turbulence. For believers who are in personal turbulence, the challenge is to remember that God is taking us to a higher altitude. God doesn't save us and move on. He loves us as we are but doesn't leave us as we are. He is shaping us, maturing us, strengthening us, taking us places. James, the brother of Jesus, put it this way:

> Consider it pure joy, my brothers and sisters, whenever you
> face trials of many kinds, because you know that the testing
> of your faith produces perseverance. Let perseverance finish

its work so that you may be mature and complete, not lacking anything.

JAMES 1:2–4

When life gets turbulent the believer does not need to panic or make demands of God. The believer remains seated and listens to God's voice. Because God is the pilot. He knows how to fly the plane. And the believer knows that if the plane is better off in smoother air, the pilot will fly the plane there. Even if not right away. God the pilot knows best.

I am not saying this kind of trust is easy. It requires us to give up control and trust Jesus at a deep level. The problem is that most believers are control freaks just like I am. We don't want to let go and trust Jesus so deeply. We want to steer. We want to fly the plane. Remember that Christian bumper sticker that said "God is my copilot"? That's a nice sentiment. People driving those cars believe, or are saying they believe, that God is backing them up, looking out for them, pitching in when necessary. This all sounds fine, but it's really bad theology. (If your doctrine is based on Christian bumper stickers, you're in trouble.) God is not a copilot. He does not play second fiddle to anyone. He is either your pilot or he is not. You either submit and trust him with your whole life, or you live nervously in the mistaken belief that you are in control.

When you acknowledge that God is your pilot, it helps you remain calm during the turbulent times. You know there is nothing else you can do except trust him. Even if you wanted to help, you would not know where to begin because you don't know how to fly the plane. So you let go and let the pilot do his thing. That is scary at first, but it is also freeing.

Jesus Responds

In our story, John the Baptist is in prison and getting impatient and frustrated. John was a religious guy, about as religious as they come. He did all the right things. He obeyed God's plan for his life—to live in the desert and preach repentance and the coming of the Messiah. He sacrificed comfort and luxury. As far as we know, he never married. But he finds himself in prison because he did what was right. He knows that Jesus is the Messiah, but the longer he stares at the walls of his cell the more he doubts whether that is really true. Unable to wait any longer he sends two of his students to ask Jesus, straight up, "Are you the Messiah or not?"

But Jesus does not respond right away. This is such a Jesus move. His cousin, the great prophet John the Baptist, the man predicted in Scripture to announce the Messiah, is locked up and his faith is faltering. Some commentators believe that Jesus waited most of the day before responding. At the very least, hours may have passed before John heard back from his two students. I can relate. I can't count the number of times I have desperately wanted a direct and immediate answer from God and have not gotten one. But God wasn't ignoring me and he wasn't late. Rather, in God's wisdom he knew that a direct and immediate answer wasn't best for me. The same may have been true for John.

Instead of giving John an instant message, Jesus continued

to preach the gospel, heal people, cure their diseases, restore their sight, and cast out demons. Afterward, Jesus told John's messengers:

> Go back and report to John what you have seen and heard: The blind receive sight, the lame walk, those who have leprosy are cleansed, the deaf hear, the dead are raised, and the good news is proclaimed to the poor.
>
> LUKE 7:22

Weird answer, right? John wonders whether Jesus is the promised Messiah, but Jesus says: "Tell John about all the miracles I'm performing." That seems to miss the point of the question. It even seems a bit calloused. John is sitting in jail for obeying God's call on his life and Jesus just responds with, "Check out the miracles I'm doing."

But what sounds dismissive at first is a profoundly helpful instruction in how to respond when doubt creeps in and shakes our faith. In this brief passage Jesus gives us two instructions on how to respond when our faith is shaken.

First, Jesus directs John to Scripture. He wasn't simply letting John know about a bunch of miracles. Jesus was quoting one of the best-known prophecies concerning the Messiah, from Isaiah:

> *The Spirit of the Sovereign LORD is on me,*
> *because the LORD has anointed me*
> *to proclaim good news to the poor.*
> *He has sent me to bind up the brokenhearted,*

> to proclaim freedom for the captives
> and release from darkness for the prisoners,
> to proclaim the year of the LORD's favor
> and the day of vengeance of our God,
> to comfort all who mourn,
> and provide for those who grieve in Zion—
> to bestow on them a crown of beauty
> instead of ashes,
> the oil of joy
> instead of mourning,
> and a garment of praise
> instead of a spirit of despair.
>
> ISAIAH 61:1–3

Jesus is not bragging about his miracles. It is something other than that. Jesus is giving John hope. He is saying, "John, remember those things that Isaiah predicted the Messiah would do? I'm doing them." With John's life falling apart— imprisoned and soon to be executed—Jesus is setting John's feet on solid ground by reminding him of the unshakeable Word of God, which will never pass away. In the midst of trial, when our world seems to be coming apart at the seams, when all of the things we thought we knew about God seem to be untrue, when we just cannot get an answer from God, Jesus points us to Scripture.

When you don't hear what God is saying, go back to what he has said.

Second, Jesus instructs us to look beyond our personal circumstances. Jesus responded to John's messengers by telling them to testify to John about all the miracles that Jesus performed. In other words, even though John is in prison, it did not change the fact that God was doing a mighty work in the world through Jesus. Just because things were not working out the way John hoped did not mean that God's plans had been thwarted or that John's belief in Jesus was mistaken. In fact, the opposite was true. God was working through Jesus to save Israel and even the whole world, and it was happening right in front of John's disciples. As long as John was focused on his own situation, he would never see beyond the prison cell. But if he could broaden his perspective to see the big picture, he would discover that God was at work.

We all go through trying times, circumstances where we feel trapped, hopeless, confused, frustrated. In those times it is tempting to throw up our hands and shout, "God, are you for me or not?" In those times Jesus tells us to step back, broaden our perspective, and look to see how God is working in the lives of others. God is big, and the world he is saving is big too. If we focus only on what is just in front of us we are probably not going to see God's working around us. It can be difficult, but the more we learn about God's working in other people's lives the more faith we will have.

I often hear of people who call themselves Christians but don't participate in a local church. They like to say things like, "I love Jesus, but I don't like church." Or, "You know, where two or more are gathered in his name, he's there also, so I'm just going to stay home with my family, and we'll have our own church." Now, it is true that you do not have be a member of a local church to be a Christian. It is also true that the people who are in churches are not perfect. But they are also believers, forgiven and redeemed believers. Even if they are stumbling or at times hypocritical, God is at work in their lives.

One of the greatest blessings I get from being part of a local church is learning all the different ways in which God is at work in the world. It reminds me that God's plan is much bigger than Rich Wilkerson. My life is a piece in the puzzle, a thread in the tapestry. God is at work everywhere, in billions of lives in every country around the world. He is knitting those lives together according to his master plan. And the more stories I hear about God's work, the more of that plan I see, and the more I see the plan unfolding, the more my faith increases.

The Bible says that a chord of three strands is not easily broken. When we exchange stories of how God is working in our lives, we are strengthened. When the rough times come, and they will come, one of the best things we can do is step back and look at the bigger picture. If we focus only on the prison walls, our faith may falter, but if we can broaden our perspective, we will find hope. God is at work all the time. Our job is to see it. If we can do that we will be blessed.

BLESSED

The answer Jesus gives to John's disciples does not end with pointing out the miracles. The response gets stranger. After pointing John to Scripture, Jesus makes one of the most perplexing statements in the Bible: "Blessed is anyone who does not stumble on account of me" (Luke 7:23). In other words, we are blessed if we can maintain our faith in spite of Jesus. This is peculiar. Jesus is the author and perfecter of our faith, but this passage suggests that he might do things that might make us lose faith. What gives?

The fact is that many people love Jesus as Savior, but they are not as fond of him as Lord. They like to think of Jesus as a genie who shows up when they need him and stays hidden when they don't. But Jesus is not a genie. He is God. And the sovereign God may act in ways and for reasons that we don't understand. Again, his kingdom is larger than just my little life. I like to think that I'm pretty important—and I am important to God, as are all believers—but in the grand scheme of things my life is a vapor. Whatever role I play on the grand stage is only a supporting role. Jesus is the star. If your God only acts in ways that you can understand, you need a new God. Yours is way too small.

God acts in ways that we cannot understand. Scripture is full of examples. Consider Job. When Job was going through the worst period of his life—deaths in the family, property destruction, disease—he questioned God. He got angry with God and demanded answers. Here's how God responded:

Then the LORD spoke to Job out of the storm. He said: "Who is this that obscures my plans with words without knowledge? Brace yourself like a man; I will question you, and you shall answer me. Where were you when I laid the earth's foundation? Tell me, if you understand. Who marked off its dimensions? Surely you know! Who stretched a measuring line across it? On what were its footings set, or who laid its

cornerstone—while the morning stars sang together and all
the angels shouted for joy?"

JOB 38:1–7

God responds by reminding Job how small Job is and how
big God is. God has far greater plans than we can imagine. He
is in the process of redeeming all of creation, the entire world.
God guides us each step of our journey, but we aren't going to
know his entire plan. We couldn't. It's too big and complex.
But Jesus knows us. He knows that in our fallen state our tendency is to believe that the world around us is all the world
there is. He knows that to us our problems seem like the only
problems in the world, our pain the only pain, our distress the
only distress. He knows that when turbulence comes we can
lose faith in God. After all, if I believe that my world is the
whole world, then the God of the whole world should fix the
problems of my world. And if he doesn't, maybe he isn't who I
thought he was.

But if I recognize that my world is not the whole world
and that my life is merely part of God's great plan, I put myself
in a much better position. Jesus tells us that we are blessed
if we can keep from stumbling from the way Jesus works in
our lives. Some of our requests will be granted. Some will not.
Some of us will be healed. Others will not. We don't know
God's entire plan. We don't know how our desires fit into it.
But we are blessed if we can maintain our faith in God regardless of how He answers our prayers.

The word translated as "blessed" in Luke 7:23 can also
be translated as "happy." So if we maintain our faith in God

regardless of how he answers, we will be happy. How? How can we be happy when God doesn't act like we want him to act? Here is what I think: It is all about perspective. If my focus is solely on what is happening to me, then I'm going to be upset when things don't go my way. But if my perspective is broader than my little world, and if I'm focused on what God is doing in the big picture, I'm not going to be disappointed.

God's purpose is being accomplished. History is moving in his direction. I have read the end of the Book, and God wins. Whatever my situation, whatever the immediate setback seems to be, God is at work redeeming the world, and there is no stopping him. The more I can see that reality and the evidence of it in the world, the more content and happier I'm going to be. It doesn't mean that I'm going to smile all the time, but it means I'll probably smile more.

In Gene Edwards's book, *The Prisoner in the Third Cell*, he points out that in Luke 7 not everyone who wanted to be healed by Jesus was healed. Edwards writes:

> A sick baby will die. An epileptic child will go on having sei-
> zures as long as he lives. A fevered young girl will suffer weeks
> of pain before she regains her health. A deaf mute will spend
> the rest of his life begging at the city gate. These and many
> others, with even more tragic stories, departed the village of
> Nain that morning . . . each so downcast that words could
> not express their feelings of hopelessness. Worst of all, from
> God came no explanation concerning His ways. Many were
> healed. But not all.
>
> And blessed is he who is not offended with me.

Blessed is he who is not offended with me because that person's perspective is broader than his own little world.

Graham Wilkerson

Hands down, the most difficult thing my family faced as I was growing up was what happened to my brother Graham. There are four Wilkerson boys in the family: Jonfulton, Graham, Taylor, and me. I'm the second-oldest. Graham is the second-youngest.

Graham was born on December 29, 1986, a healthy baby. Another healthy boy. (My dad is great at a lot of things, but making girls isn't one of them.) When Graham was six months old, he got really sick, and when he wasn't getting any better my mom took him to see a doctor. The doctor said that Graham had an ear infection and there was nothing serious to worry about, so he sent Graham home. Maybe it was motherly instinct, but my mom wasn't convinced. She and Graham went to our grandmother's house, and after a few minutes there Mom decided to take Graham to the hospital.

On the way there Graham slipped into unconsciousness and then stopped breathing. At the hospital, Mom laid Graham on the nurse's station and someone yelled, "Code blue!" Medical personnel worked frantically to get Graham's heart beating again. Mom looked on helplessly. "This isn't happening!" she shouted.

This was no ear infection. What we didn't know was that Graham was suffering from spinal meningitis. Graham actually died on the operating table. For more than ten minutes he was lifeless. No heartbeat. No breath. But by the grace of God and a lot of hard work by the doctors Graham's heart started to beat again. Unfortunately, the damage was done. He had been without oxygen for so long that his brain was permanently damaged.

Graham stabilized and spent a few days in the hospital, where we were given a grim prognosis. Graham's internal systems were functioning, but he was probably going to spend the rest of his life in a vegetative state, unable to move or communicate. The doctor told us he would never walk, talk, hear, see, or care for himself. For the rest of his life he would need constant care. My parents were devastated.

Dad had flown back from a revival crusade in another state to find his son near death, his wife's faith shattered, and his older sons broken and confused. His mind was racing. What had he done to deserve this? Hadn't he served God faithfully? Hadn't he sacrificed valuable time with his family to serve God? Had he done something wrong? Was he being punished?

But God did not answer, at least not as my dad wanted.

And blessed is anyone who does not stumble on account of me.

Dad could have gotten angry with God. He could have turned away from the faith he always held. He could have led our entire family away from God. But he didn't. He clung to the truth he knew, that God was for him and had a plan for his life and for Graham's life. Dad knew that God works all things together for the good of those who love him, and that in the end sickness and death are defeated. Whatever God would or would not do with Graham, the story was not over. Dad did not stumble. He kept his sight on God, not on our family's horrific circumstances. And he was blessed with faith that led us through our family's most trying days.

I wish I could tell you that Graham was miraculously and completely healed and that the doctors were baffled and could only credit God for Graham's healing. But I can't. Graham did get better, however, much better, but he was never 100 percent again. The severe brain damage has entirely altered his life. But the doctor was wrong about Graham's future. He can walk, see, hear, and even talk (with some difficulty). He still requires additional care, but he continues to progress.

In more ways than one Graham is a success story. He brings smiles to hundreds of people every week at our church just by being Graham. He loves to joke around. He loves to dance. He loves to rap. Yes, rap! He's amazing. I'm so thankful that God saved Graham's life and allowed us to have him all these years. I'm even more grateful that by God's grace my father did not stumble back then. If he had, I'm not sure I would be where I am today, serving the God of the universe in some of the most fun and rewarding ways possible.

And blessed is anyone who does not stumble on account of me.

Amen to that.

In God We Trust

In all of this the key question for all of us, just as it was for John the Baptist, is simple: "Do we trust God?" When the going gets tough, it is not about simply believing in God. The question is not "Do you believe that God exists?" or "Do you believe that Jesus is the Son of God?" The question is, "Do you trust God?" Belief is important, but in the darkest days it is trust that gives us hope. I like the following illustration about the difference between belief and trust.

Charles Blondin was a French tightrope walker and acrobat. In the 1800s, Blondin became famous for his death-defying stunts. Perhaps his most famous one was walking a tightrope across the Niagara Gorge.

I've been to Niagara Falls, and it's not the kind of water you want to mess around with. The falls are over 3,000 feet wide and 165 feet high. More than 75,000 gallons of water flow over the falls every second. The water hits the bottom with over 2,500 tons of force. You don't want to fall in.

In 1858, Blondin got the bright idea to put a tightrope over Niagara and walk across. The rope stretched 1,100 feet from end to end and was approximately 160 feet over the water. When an anxious crowd gathered to see him walk across, or plummet to certain death, Blondin stepped onto the rope and wowed the crowd by walking across.

He did this many more times on many more days. And as any good showman, Blondin changed the performance from time to time to keep it fresh. For example, he walked across blindfolded and also on stilts. On one occasion he pushed a wheelbarrow across the tightrope. When he reached the other side the crowd went wild. They cheered and celebrated this acrobat and his amazing talent.

In the midst of the cheering Blondin shouted to the crowd, "How many of you believe I can make it back to the other side?" Everyone said, "We believe! We believe!" Blondin grinned and then said, "Wonderful! Now, who will ride in the wheelbarrow back with me?" Suddenly the crowd was silent. No one was willing to ride in the wheelbarrow. They knew that Blondin could do it. They just weren't sure he could do it with one of them along for the ride. They believed, but they didn't trust.

Trust goes beyond belief. Trust means saying, "Jesus, I'm going to jump into the wheelbarrow and know that you will get me to the other side. I know it's windy. I know the water is raging. I know the rope will sway. I know that we might fall. But I am placing my life in your hands. And if we fall I know that you know what is best." That is trust.

Religion tells us to believe. Believe this doctrine. Believe these truths. Believe this dogma. But a relationship with Jesus goes deeper than mere belief. Relationship requires trust. And when we trust Jesus, regardless of the circumstances, we are blessed.

One of my favorite hymns is "'Tis So Sweet to Trust in Jesus." It was written by Louisa M. R. Stead. The story behind the song is what makes it so special.

On a sunny day, Louisa and her husband took their family on a picnic. As they were enjoying the day, their peaceful picnic was interrupted by a loud scream. They looked toward the water and saw a boy drowning nearby. Quickly, Mr. Stead got up and dived into the water to save the boy. He reached him, but the boy struggled. He fought and clawed and grabbed Mr. Stead, eventually pulling him under the water. As Louisa and her daughter stood helplessly by, the boy and Mr. Stead went under the water one last time, and they both drowned.

With her husband gone, Louisa and her daughter eventually fell into extreme poverty. They were destitute. But through it all Louisa maintained her faith in God. She knew that God never left her side. He met her needs in the most amazing ways, and in 1882, Louisa penned these beautiful lyrics about what it is like to trust God, no matter what:

'Tis so sweet to trust in Jesus,
Just to take Him at His Word,
Just to rest upon His promise,
Just to know, "Thus says the Lord!"
Jesus, Jesus, how I trust Him!
How I've proved Him o'er and o'er!
Jesus, Jesus, precious Jesus!
O for grace to trust Him more!
O how sweet to trust in Jesus,
Just to trust His cleansing blood,
Just in simple faith to plunge me
'Neath the healing, cleansing flood!
Yes, 'tis sweet to trust in Jesus,
Just from sin and self to cease,
Just from Jesus simply taking
Life and rest, and joy and peace.

I'm so glad I learned to trust Him,
Precious Jesus, Savior, Friend;
And I know that He is with me,
Will be with me to the end.

Chapter Nine

GOSSIP GOD

*After John's messengers left, Jesus began to speak to the crowd
about John: "What did you go out into the wilderness to see?
A reed swayed by the wind? If not, what did you go out to see?
A man dressed in fine clothes? No, those who wear expensive
clothes and indulge in luxury are in palaces. But what did
you go out to see? A prophet? Yes, I tell you, and more than
a prophet. This is the one about whom it is written:
"'I will send my messenger ahead of you,
who will prepare your way before you.'
I tell you, among those born of women there is no
one greater than John; yet the one who is least in
the kingdom of God is greater than he."*

LUKE 7:24–28

Working Out Doesn't Always Work Out

There are things in life you don't want to do, but you just have to do them—mowing grass, washing dishes, eating spinach, and the one I hate most, working out. Seriously, I hate it. I know, I know. Many people love working out. They say things like, "I love the rush! The endorphins are such a high!" I have no idea what they're talking about. Nothing about working out excites me. I don't feel endorphins when I work out. I feel hot, sweaty, exhausted, and a fair amount of pain.

I know I need to work out, but I always look for any excuse not to. If there's a reason not to work out, any reason at all, I won't. Sometimes I arrive at the gym and, oops, I don't have my headphones. Can't work out without headphones, right? How am I supposed to hear that epic workout playlist I put together? Might as well head home and try again tomorrow. The next day I'll arrive without my water bottle. No way am I working out without properly hydrating. That's medically dangerous. Any excuse will do—broken air conditioning at the gym, too many people, too few people, no spotter, I'm too busy that day. Whatever. Maybe you can relate. Or maybe you're one of those crazy endorphin people. If so, God bless you, but we probably won't be friends.

One of the biggest issues I have is how crowded the gym

usually is. Well, that's not entirely accurate. My problem isn't with the crowd (except when I'm looking for an excuse to leave). My problem is that the crowd is full of guys who are in ridiculously good shape. They're shredded, just ripped. They have muscles upon muscles. I wonder sometimes whether those guys just live at the gym. Do they have jobs? How in the world can people be that fit? Do they sleep? Are they working out in their sleep?

Someone needs to tell these guys the mission has been accomplished. They look great. They don't need to keep showing up at the gym and reminding the rest of us how out of shape we are. I admit it. I'm self-conscious around these guys. I feel peer pressure from them, even though they probably could care less about me. I'm sure they don't even care that I'm there, unless I'm between them and the mirror they're using to admire their six packs. I always feel like they are judging me and sizing up my weakness. This can lead me into problems.

One time, I was doing a military press. That's the one where you sit down and push the weights from shoulder-height up over your head. After a few reps, paranoia set in. No one said anything to me, but I could just feel the judgmental glances from the steroid—oops, sorry—muscle crowd. I was just certain they were watching and thinking, "Rich, are you serious? That's all you can put up? You can't be that weak."

In my foolish pride, I then thought, "I can do a lot more than this. I'll show them." So I grabbed some heavier dumbbells, weights that I had never lifted before, and I pushed those bad boys right up over my head. For the first two reps I felt like the man, but on the third press my body gave up on me. A knife-like sensation started in my lower back and worked its way right up to my neck. It was excruciating. I had pinched a nerve.

Immediately I dropped the weights, but I tried to look tough doing it, like I threw down the weights because I had just conquered them. I stared at them with angry eyebrows and did that weird "shoo, shoo" breathing thing that people do when they work out extra hard. But I didn't feel very tough. My neck was completely locked up, totally stiff. I couldn't turn it. There was no way I could keep exercising. I left the gym looking like Beaker from the Muppets. (Remember Beaker? He wore a lab coat and had crazy orange hair. He also didn't have a neck.) My neck was stiff for days. It was painful. I would hear people call my name and I had to turn my whole body around to see who it was. But at least I showed the steroid crowd.

I injured myself when I tried to lift a weight that was too heavy for me, and my injury slowed me down for weeks. How many people try to carry weights they were never intended to carry and end up hurt? How many people's lives are inhibited because they're carrying weights that are too heavy? How many are living with injuries suffered from trying to carry what they were never intended to carry?

Religion, as we saw in an earlier chapter, is not bad in itself, but it can become a weight too heavy to carry. And the more we try to carry that crushing weight, the more likely we are to be injured and the stiffer we may become. Religion can become so rigid that it becomes lifeless. That kind of religion is a burden we were not meant to carry. That's why Jesus said in Matthew 11:28–30: "Come to me, all you who are weary and burdened, and I will give you rest. Take my yoke upon you and learn from me, for I am gentle and humble in heart, and you will find rest for your souls. For my yoke is easy and my burden is light."

Jesus, of course, was not talking about physical burdens. He was referring to the crushing religious system of works-based righteousness that the Pharisees required of the Jewish people. In Jesus' day the Pharisees taught that people had to obey all of the Law in order to be in good standing with God. They insisted on legalistic rule-keeping and imposed onerous regulations on the people.

For example, the Law commanded that people were not to work on the Sabbath. It was a day of rest. Some scholars believe that the Pharisees had over six hundred regulations concerning what qualified as working on the Sabbath. Talk about a burden! Imagine having to review six hundred regulations today in order to decide whether you can mow your yard on Sunday without getting in trouble with God. The Pharisees were overburdened with religion, and since they were the religious authorities they imposed that crushing burden—their rules and regulations—on others. No wonder the people were "weary and burdened."

Thank God for Jesus. He came to remove this heavy burden. It's no longer about what we do. It's about what he has done. He did not bring more regulations. He brought a resolution. He did not bring a reminder of our sins. He brought the remission for our sins. He fulfilled the old covenant and all of its laws and established the new covenant where we find rest. Jesus' yoke is easy and his burden is light.

Behind His Back

How much weight must John the Baptist have been carrying? Imprisoned, waiting to die, doubting who Jesus was and perhaps losing his faith. I wonder if he questioned his behavior. Have I fallen short? Is God punishing me for some sin? As we saw, John sent two of his disciples to ask Jesus whether he was the true Messiah. As we saw earlier, Jesus responded with those perplexing (but profound) words, "Blessed is he who does not stumble on account of me."

The next part of the story is equally fascinating. After Jesus sends John's disciples back to John, Jesus addresses the crowd. He talks to them about John. Now John probably won't ever hear what Jesus said about him, because he's in prison and isn't going to get out. Basically, Jesus is talking behind John's back.

Most of the time when someone talks behind your back it's not a good thing. Usually it's something they would never say to your face. It might be a rumor or, worse, slander. Whatever it is, usually it ain't good. But this is Jesus we're talking about, and no one believes in our potential more than the One who created us.

Jesus asks the crowd why they went out into the desert to see John. What were they looking for? Certainly they weren't looking for a rich celebrity. No, they wanted to see a man marked by God, a true prophet. And not just any prophet. Luke 7:27 tells us that they wanted to see the prophet that Malachi had written about hundreds of years earlier:

> I will send my messenger ahead of you,
> who will prepare your way before you.

Then Jesus tells the crowd something amazing. Jesus says that John is the greatest man ever born of a woman. Talk about a compliment! Jesus, the King of kings and Lord of lords, calls John the greatest man to ever live.

Think about what is going on here. John is doubting whether Jesus is the true Messiah. In our day if a pastor openly questioned whether Jesus is the Messiah he would probably lose his job. But Jesus doesn't condemn John for his doubt. Instead, Jesus affirms him. Isn't that fascinating?

Have you ever wondered what Jesus is doing when he seems far away? Have you ever wondered what he is saying when you can't hear him? Have you ever wondered what he is thinking when you're having doubts? In John's case, when he is doubting Jesus, Jesus is bragging on John.

Jesus wasn't angry with John. He loved John, even in John's worst moments, because Jesus' relationship with John was not based on John's emotions or state of mind. The relationship was based on Jesus' love for John, and that love would never be shaken. A relationship with Jesus is so much better than a burdensome religion, which condemns us when we are down. But Jesus loves us always, even when we are down.

A man once approached Jesus, desperate for his help. Mark 9:14–27 explains that the man's son was being tormented by a demon, which no one had been able to do anything about. The man begged Jesus for help. Jesus responded by saying that anything is possible for one who believes. The man replied, "I do believe; help me overcome my unbelief!"

Poor man. He believed that Jesus was special. He believed that Jesus had supernatural power. But he also knew that no one had been able to help his son. He hoped, but he also doubted. Can you relate? You might think Jesus was insulted by the man's doubt. Maybe he would even delay the miracle until the man was full of faith. But Jesus did not respond as if he had been insulted, and he didn't procrastinate. Instantly, Jesus drove the spirit out and healed the man's son.

Paul tells us in 2 Timothy 2:13, "If we are faithless, he remains faithful, for he cannot disown himself." Even when we are faithless, Jesus is still faithful. He doesn't just love us; he is love. He doesn't just treat us kindly; he is kindness. He doesn't just give us joy; he is joy. Whatever we do, Jesus won't change his nature.

John is at his lowest moment. The wild, fiery prophet, so used to the freedom of the wilderness, has become locked in a cold, dark cell. He spent his ministry proclaiming the coming of the Messiah, and yet in prison, when his world was turned upside down, he doubted Jesus' identity. Many would mock John. Some would ridicule him. Others might even call him a traitor. But not Jesus. He called John the greatest man who ever lived.

GOD KNOWS YOU

Did you know that you are on God's mind? Did you know that you are not an inconsequential speck of creation that God made long ago and never thought of again? Did you know that he knows you intimately (better than you know yourself) and that he cares deeply about your life? Did you know that he talks about you?

My favorite chapter in the book of Psalms is 139. It's a beautifully written lyric regarding God's intimate participation in our lives. The first six verses tell us so much about how God thinks about us.

> You have searched me, LORD,
> and you know me.
> You know when I sit and when I rise;
> you perceive my thoughts from afar.
> You discern my going out and my lying down;
> you are familiar with all my ways.
> Before a word is on my tongue
> you, LORD, know it completely.
> You hem me in behind and before,
> and you lay your hand upon me.
> Such knowledge is too wonderful for me,
> too lofty for me to attain.
>
> PSALM 139:1–6

Have you ever met a know-it-all, a person who loves to give advice even though you never asked for it? One time I was shopping at the mall, trying on some clothes. Out of nowhere one of the sales clerks looked at the shirt I had tried on and said, "That is so not your color." She was probably right, but I bought the shirt anyway, just to spite her. I didn't care that she works in the fashion world and probably knows what looks good on certain people and what does not. Her unsolicited knowledge of the fashion industry didn't matter to me because we didn't know each other. It reminded me of an old saying:

"People don't care how much you know until they know how much you care."

When it comes to your life, Jesus knows it all. Go back and reread the Psalm above. God searches us. That means he examines us, studies us. And as a result, he knows us. He knows our habits. He knows our thoughts. He knows when we go and when we rest. He knows everything about us, even what we will say before we say it. He knows us completely.

There is a big difference between meeting someone and knowing someone. When I was in high school, my friend Jason told me he knew Scottie Pippen, one of the greatest basketball players in the world. He and his teammate Michael Jordan were unstoppable when I was growing up. They were the dynamic duo, like Batman and Robin, Snoopy and Charlie Brown, the Lone Ranger and Tonto.

Apparently Jason's dad had done some business with Scottie, so one day Scottie took Jason and his dad to play a round of golf. But when Jason said that he knew Scottie, I didn't believe him for a second. He told me he would prove it by taking me to a game and introducing me. I went along with it. We went to the game, and as it ended Jason worked his way through the crowd and slipped past the security guard and on to the floor. He had a T-shirt in his hand and was waving it above his head like a helicopter, shouting at the top of his lungs, "Scottie! Scottie!" Scottie was leaving the court and walking toward the tunnel. He looked in Jason's direction, but when he saw him he just kept walking.

Jason walked back up the stairs to me and said, "He didn't see me." Being the mean friend that I am, I called him out.

"Of course he saw you," I said. "He just doesn't know you. Just because you met him once doesn't mean that he knows you." There's a big difference between an acquaintance and a friend.

In God's eyes, you are not just some acquaintance. He knows everything about you. The psalmist says, "Lord, you have searched me and you know me." Have you ever been searched? One time my mom and I had the amazing opportunity to visit the White House. It was an incredible experience. We were invited to a presidential Christmas party. Before entering the White House, we had to go through security. We were searched. I mean *really* searched. They went through everything in my bag. They did a complete pat-down. There was some invasion of privacy, as in, some private areas were invaded. But hey, it was the president.

God has searched you up and down, backward and forward, inside and out. Nothing is hidden from him. God knows you.

Consider what it means for God to know you. He is the Creator of the heavens and the earth. He is the author of life and death. He is the beginning and the end, the Alpha and the Omega. He is so big, and yet he knows everything there is to know about little ol' you. He knows your dreams, your desires, your wants, your appetites, your tendencies, everything about you.

GOD CONCENTRATES ON YOU

Look again at the Psalm:

You know when I sit and when I rise;
you perceive my thoughts from afar.
You discern my going out and my lying down;
you are familiar with all my ways.
Before a word is on my tongue
you, LORD, know it completely.

PSALM 139:2–4

It is not just that God knows you. He focuses on you. He concentrates on you. He did not just Google some facts about you. He watches you. He studies you. He cherishes you. The psalmist gives us a detailed description of God's focus on us, almost as if God is consumed with us.

Have you tried to have a conversation with someone who was distracted? You're trying to connect but they won't get off their phone or put down the remote. It's frustrating because they aren't focusing on you. It seems as if they don't care.

That is not God. He is not preoccupied with something else. He has all the time in the world for you. David says, "You know when I sit and when I rise." What he means is that God watches our every move. God watches us coming and going. He even watches when we wake up and we go to sleep. The other day I woke up and my wife was just looking at me. She said, "I love watching you sleep." Friend, you are precious to God. He loves you. He even likes to watch you sleep.

The psalm also says that God is familiar with all your ways. You might be thinking, "Wait a minute. I'm cool with God knowing some of my ways, but all my ways? What about last Friday? You know I didn't mean it." Yet God loves you, even knowing all of your blemishes—the good, the bad, and the ugly. You can't do anything to make him love you more or love you less. If he loves you today you can rest assured that he will love you tomorrow. He knows what you did, what you didn't do, and what you're going do. And he is going to love you.

Have you ever known someone so well that you knew what they were thinking without their ever saying a word? This is how well God knows us. Scripture says that before a word is on my tongue, God already knows it.

God concentrates on you. The question is, are you aware of him?

If God is so focused, why are we so distracted? God wants to communicate with us. He wants to speak to us. Actually, he is constantly speaking to us. Many of us just don't want to hear what he is saying. You may think that God has gone silent, when the reality is that he is waiting for you to respond to what he has already said. Whenever I don't know what to do next, I always do the last thing he told me to do. I find that the more I obey, the more wonderful things he gives me to do.

GOD IS FOR YOU

God knows me and concentrates on me. But it doesn't stop there. God is for me!

> *You hem me in behind and before,*
> *and you lay your hand upon me.*
>
> PSALM 139:5

God protects you. He has a plan for your life. He has a purpose for you in his kingdom. God has surrounded you and
placed his hand upon you. He is all around you, doing for you
what you cannot do for yourself. He lays his hand upon you.

When this psalm was written it was accepted practice
that when someone "blessed" another person, he laid his hand
upon the person when doing that. When a father blessed his
son by giving him his inheritance, he would do so by placing
his hand upon him. The laying on of hands symbolized blessing, power, and inheritance.

There are a lot of things I can do without in this life. I can
do without a lot of money. I can do without power. I can do
without fame. But I can't do without God's hand on my life. I
need his blessing. I need his favor.

If God is for you, who can be against you? With God, you
are the majority. No weapon formed against you will prosper.
You are more than a conqueror. Enemies will rise up. Betrayers
will emerge. Haters will try to tear you down. Doubters will
talk about you. The whole world might be against you. But if
God is for you, who can be against you?

Then the psalm states what we are probably all thinking
now: "Such knowledge is too wonderful for me, too lofty for
me to attain" (Psalm 139:6).

How can it be that the God of the universe would care
about us, would study us and know us, and that despite knowing everything that there is to know about us (our sins, our
weaknesses, our shame), still be for us? It is too wonderful
to understand. The psalmist can't comprehend God, but he
chooses to trust him. Can you trust God? When he tells you

to hold on, when he tells you to wait, when he tells you it's not your turn, when he tells you no, can you trust him? Let's start living by God's promises instead of waiting for his explanations. His promises are enough.

Part Four

THE OUTCAST

*When one of the Pharisees invited Jesus to have dinner with
him, he went to the Pharisee's house and reclined at the table.
A woman in that town who lived a sinful life learned that Jesus
was eating at the Pharisee's house, so she came there with an
alabaster jar of perfume. As she stood behind him at his feet
weeping, she began to wet his feet with her tears. Then she wiped
them with her hair, kissed them and poured perfume on them.
When the Pharisee who had invited him saw this, he said to
himself, "If this man were a prophet, he would know who is touching
him and what kind of woman she is—that she is a sinner."
Jesus answered him, "Simon, I have something to tell you."
"Tell me, teacher," he said.
"Two people owed money to a certain moneylender. One
owed him five hundred denarii, and the other fifty. Neither
of them had the money to pay him back, so he forgave the
debts of both. Now which of them will love him more?"
Simon replied, "I suppose the one who had the bigger debt forgiven."*

"You have judged correctly," Jesus said.

Then he turned toward the woman and said to Simon, "Do you see this woman? I came into your house. You did not give me any water for my feet, but she wet my feet with her tears and wiped them with her hair. You did not give me a kiss, but this woman, from the time I entered, has not stopped kissing my feet. You did not put oil on my head, but she has poured perfume on my feet. Therefore, I tell you, her many sins have been forgiven—as her great love has shown. But whoever has been forgiven little loves little."

Then Jesus said to her, "Your sins are forgiven."

The other guests began to say among themselves, "Who is this who even forgives sins?"

Jesus said to the woman, "Your faith has saved you; go in peace."

LUKE 7:36–50

Chapter Ten

THE WOMAN
WITH NO NAME

When one of the Pharisees invited Jesus to have dinner
with him, he went to the Pharisee's house and reclined
at the table. A woman in that town who lived a sinful
life learned that Jesus was eating at the Pharisee's house,
so she came there with an alabaster jar of perfume.

LUKE 7:36–37

Renting vs. Owning

One of my favorite things in the entire world is to stay at a nice hotel. Not a motel. Definitely not a hostel, which I'm pretty sure is where we got the word "hostage." No, I'm talking about a hotel, and a nice one, where the rooms have a big, beautiful bed and fluffy comforter and pillows, and where they leave those little pieces of expensive chocolate for you every night. The place has twenty-four-hour room service. Come on, who doesn't love room service? You pick up the phone, order, and a guy brings food to your bedroom! You can have breakfast in bed every day. And lunch. And dinner. There's a pool, a gym, a spa, at least one restaurant, and my favorite thing of all, housekeeping. Honestly, sometimes I wonder if maybe God has called me to live in a nice hotel. Bellhops need Jesus too, you know.

Nice hotels are fantastic, so fantastic that people can lose their minds in them. It's hilarious. All right, maybe they don't lose their minds, but they're certainly careless. For example, the shower you take is always extra long. You just let the water run. You are not paying the water bill, right? It is built into the price of the room. Gotta get your money's worth!

When you finally finish your hour-long tropical shower treatment, what do you do? You don't hang the towel on that little hook like a civilized person. No, you toss it on the floor like you're spiking a football. It should be fine there, all balled up in the corner, sopping wet, just growing mildew. Then you grab a slice of "coal-fired pizza" and slip into bed. After all, the best place to eat coal-fired pizza is under the covers, washed down with a diet cola. My wife and I recently got into a pillow fight at a hotel. Who still gets into pillow fights? We do! But only in hotels, when we are allowed to be careless.

We are more prone to be more careless with things we don't own. I don't treat my house the way I treat a hotel. I own my house, and because of that I take care of it. I hang up my clothes. I put the TV remote in its proper place. I hang up the towel. I even make my bed. There is no maid. (When I got married I thought DawnCheré was going to do most of that stuff. Boy was I wrong!) Why do I do all these things at home? Because I own it. I bought it for a price. It cost me something. I'm not just renting. It will be mine for a long time. When you own something you take care of it.

God reminds us in 1 Corinthians 6:19–20 that our salvation cost him greatly: "You are not your own; you were bought at a price." Jesus paid the price for your past, present, and future sins. He bought you at a price. What was the price? He laid down his life on a cruel cross. His blood purchased your destiny. He is not renting you. He bought you. And because he bought you, he treats you carefully. He has a plan for you. It is not a careless plan. It is a careful one. The more we recognize how much God paid for us, the more we love and worship. The more we become aware of all that he did, the closer to him we get. He is not careless. He is careful.

A SINFUL WOMAN

In our fourth, and final, story of Luke 7, we meet a woman to whom, in one way or another, we all can relate. Here's how the story goes.

Jesus is invited over to a Pharisee's house for dinner. I love reading that Jesus is hanging out with a Pharisee. Pharisees get a bad rap in Christianity. We like to beat up on Pharisees. They are the legalistic, religious hypocrites who had the Romans crucify Jesus. But they were also people. And Jesus loved people. All people. In this story, Jesus hangs out at a Pharisee's house. Most of us know that Jesus has grace for the prodigal, but did you know that he has grace for the Pharisee too? Jesus did not come just for those who committed the crime. He also came for those who judged the crime. He can save the offender and the judge alike.

When Jesus arrives at the house he reclines at the table. I love this picture. Can't you just imagine Jesus reclining there, leaning back like a boss? I know that reclining at the table on pillows was a cultural thing, instead of sitting on chairs as we do today, but I prefer to think of Jesus as the inventor of swag. He walks into the room, leans back, and starts spittin' truth. If Jesus drove a car, I imagine he would be one of those guys with the seat laid way back, music bumpin', and just cruising around.

Anyway, so a woman walks in unannounced and uninvited. The host is embarrassed that she is there because this woman is not part of respectable society. The Bible does not record her name. She is known simply as "the sinful woman."

That's pretty rough. Can you imagine what it would be like if people knew you only by the sins you have committed? No one knows your name. They only know you by your sins. Your sins are your identity.

Imagine meeting people. Someone asks, "What's your name?" You reply, "I'm Greed." (Or fill in the blank with the sin of your choice: lust, gossip, drunkenness, anger, gluttony, whatever.) People would look at you with disdain and judgment. You would be ridiculed and avoided.

On the other hand, maybe it would help in some situations. Take dating, for example. Some dude hollers at a girl. "You're cute. What's your name?" She looks him in the eye and tells him, straight up, "I'm Cheater." I am guessing that dude would break off the hand shake and give her an, "Alrighty, then. I'm outta here."

We don't identify ourselves by our shortcomings. No one I know is walking up to people and introducing themselves as "Worrier" or "Adulterer" or "Abuser." We don't label ourselves that way, but we sure do it to each other. I see it all the time, people categorized by their mistakes and behavior. They become their mistake.

This is a reason why many people avoid church at all costs. Even those who have messed up, repented, and accepted God's grace still may find it hard to shake the bad reputation they earned before meeting Jesus when they are around "church people." They are often reminded of what they once were instead of who they now are.

I have heard it said that Christians are the only people who kill their own wounded. I hate that thought. It means that we hurt our own people, our brothers and sisters, who are coming to us for help. What if there were a hospital that welcomed all people but only treated some? What if there were some diseases that were considered so bad that, instead of treating those people, the doctors gave them drugs that made their pain worse or killed them? How crazy would that be? Yet in churches across our nation this happens every week. Wounded people show up needing love and grace and kindness, and instead they experience raised eyebrows, harsh words, judgmental glances, and suspicion.

People wear masks at church because they are afraid to show their true selves, for fear of being judged or rejected. Sometimes I wonder what would happen if Mary, the mother of Jesus, walked into some of our churches today, fifteen years old and pregnant. I imagine her being greeted by a gaggle of ladies all smiling and saying hello, but as she walked away to take her seat in the sanctuary, my guess is that at least one of the women would look at the others and whisper, "That's Mary. She's gotten herself pregnant. Says the father is the Holy Spirit. Bless her heart. Y'all be praying for her."

The sinful woman in Luke 7 probably felt like this at times. The glances, the judgmental stares. She knew the sting of being a social outcast, a less-than. Most theologians believe that she was a prostitute, but whatever her sin, it gave her a bad reputation. Who knows how she ended up in this predicament? My guess is that she never planned on being there. Little girls don't grow up dreaming about selling their bodies to pay the bills. But in all likelihood, that's where she was. Night after night men rented her body. No one was careful with her. She was used to people being careless. This was the woman with no name.

She Learns

The Bible says that the woman with no name learned that Jesus was in town. By this time, Jesus' reputation was huge. He was famous—as famous as an ancient rabbi could be. The woman did not know Jesus yet. But somehow she knew of him. What must she have heard? Did she hear that Jesus had healing powers? Did she hear that the religious establishment considered him dangerous? Did she hear that he was claiming to be able to forgive sins? Did she hear that he was delivering people from bondage and giving them freedom? We don't know what people told her about Jesus, but it was enough, enough to make her think, enough to make her wonder, enough to make her ask, "What if any of this is true?"

Have you ever invited someone to church many times but he or she never came? Or what about the time the person finally came, but the main pastor was not preaching, or he was talking about something really deep or weird that day: "Open your Bible to Ezekiel." And you're like, "Dang it!" Or the preacher says, "Today, we're going to talk about demonology." And you look at your friend and say, "It's really never like this, I promise."

Or maybe you tried to tell someone about Jesus and got rejected. And you thought, "I'm no good at this whole witnessing thing." At times like that, I'm reminded of what Paul writes in 1 Corinthians 3:6: "I planted the seed. Apollos watered it, but God has been making it grow." As believers, our job is not to save people. It is not even to persuade them that we are right. Our job is simply to plant and water the seed. Jesus makes the seed grow.

When I was growing up, we kids would go grocery shopping with our mom. There were four boys, so we went to Costco and bought in bulk. In a house with four boys, it's nice to have a gallon-sized tub of mayonnaise. It makes sense to buy toilet paper by the pallet. And who would buy a dozen eggs when you can get four dozen at a time?

What I loved about Costco was the sample corners, little areas where they offered small samples of food. My brothers and I would get a full meal just from circling the sample areas. Our favorite was pizza bites. I remember the first time I tried those little pieces of manna. The moment I got a taste I was sold. I couldn't stop thinking about them. Of course I nagged my mom all the way around the store until she bought some.

Here's the deal. Jesus' followers have to be willing to give people a taste of who Jesus is. When people get a sample of how good Jesus is, it leaves them wanting more. Maybe that is why Psalm 34:8 says: "Taste and see that the LORD is good." We don't have to be the smartest, the sharpest, or the most talented. We don't have to have all the answers. We just have to be willing to give people a little taste of who Jesus is.

Someone had given the sinful woman in Luke 7 a taste of who Jesus was. She had learned that Jesus was in town, so she made her way to the house and went in. Someone had been giving her samples, but now she has a chance to get the whole thing. This broken woman was on her way to being made whole. And she wasn't taking no for an answer.

THE WORLD

We can only speculate about her background and how she ended up with a bad reputation. Maybe she had a bad upbringing. Maybe her parents were not around during her formative years. Maybe they were terrible parents. Maybe they did everything right. Maybe her family was rich. Maybe it was poor. Maybe she was educated, but most likely she was not. My point is that we normally can't control what happens around us, but we usually can control how we respond.

We each make choices every day. Today's reality was shaped by yesterday's choices, and tomorrow we will experience the consequences of the choices we make today. It's a simple principle, but one we often forget. Our lives are largely the result of the choices we make. We don't know exactly what choices led this sinful woman to have a bad reputation, but odds are that, at some point, she began believing that the world could make her happy. If she could just make enough money, just get the right man's affection, just achieve a little more social status, then surely she would be happy.

In this final section I want to examine the story of the sinful woman by focusing especially on the sandy foundation that we Christians call "the world." I know, that's a churchy word, and it can be a confusing one. After all, how can we not build our lives on the world? Don't we live in the world? Don't we survive because of the world?

Here is what I mean when I say we shouldn't build our lives on the world. God made a good creation. When the first humans sinned, God's creation was corrupted, but good things remained: beauty, pleasure, food, companionship, and countless others. God created people to enjoy the good things he made even after the first humans sinned. The problem comes when we start worshiping one of these created things instead of the Creator. When we care more about the good things God has made than we care about God, we are headed for disappointment.

The apostle John warns us about this. I like how *The Message* translates it:

> Don't love the world's ways. Don't love the world's goods. Love of the world squeezes out love for the Father. Practically everything that goes on in the world—wanting your own way, wanting everything for yourself, wanting to appear important—has nothing to do with the Father. It just isolates you from him. The world and all its wanting, wanting, wanting is on the way out—but whoever does what God wants is set for eternity.
>
> 1 JOHN 2:15–17

John is telling us that the world's plan for our lives doesn't line up with God's plan. The world wants us to settle down and only think about ourselves—to eat, drink, and be merry, for tomorrow we die. The world does not see beyond today. It is all about the moment. If it feels good, do it. If it sounds good, go for it. If it tastes good, eat it. Sounds great, right? And it can be great, for a while. But the funny thing about appetites is that the more you feed them, the stronger they get. The world can deliver success, power, and pleasure, but those things are never enough. There is no such thing as enough success, enough power, or enough pleasure. It is like trying to catch the horizon. You'll never get there.

One of my favorite hobbies is going to the movies. (We can debate some other time whether or not that is a real hobby. It is for me.) For me, going to the movies is a production. I have a whole process. I arrive twenty minutes early to stop at the concession stand and get a frozen cola, a medium popcorn, and a bag of the world's greatest candy, Twizzlers. (We will not be debating the superiority of Twizzlers. That is beyond dispute.) Then I take a seat in the theater at least ten minutes before show time, because I absolutely have to see the previews. Previews are awesome. Think about it. They sum up a two-hour movie in two minutes. All of the highlights are crammed into one fantastic sequence. The score is on point, the voice-over guy with the gravelly baritone is epic, and you are on the edge of your seat the whole time. It's all so perfect. I don't remember the last time I saw a preview and didn't immediately think, "I have to see that movie!"

Unfortunately, more times than not, the actual movie turns out to be nowhere near as good as the preview. Why? Because the preview promised something that the movie could not deliver. It is the same with sin. It looks great from the outside, and when we get a little taste it makes us hungry for more. But in the end it leaves us empty and unsatisfied. And often, instead of turning away from sin, we choose to taste it again, thinking maybe this time it will be different. "If I just drink a little more . . . If I just smoke this . . . If I can just get with her . . ." But the end result is the same. Sin always takes us further than we want to go, and it keeps us there longer than we want to stay.

Sin always leads to more sin. A little bit of yeast works its way through the whole batch of dough. Think about Adam and Eve. They were banished from the garden of Eden because they ate some forbidden fruit. And Adam's son, Cain, murders his brother Abel. It seems like a huge leap to go from eating the wrong fruit to homicide, but sin leads to more sin. Small sin leads to big sin. A little sin leads to more sin.

The sinful woman with no name in Luke 7 represents a person who trusts in the world. Somewhere in her story she believed the lie. We are often amazed to see a person's life collapse. We wonder how the disaster developed. Often, it is one compromise after another. How did this woman end up on the streets selling her body for sex? She compromised who she was created to be. She traded her integrity for a quick fix. She chose the here and now and disregarded the future that she was designed for.

Building a life on the world will always leave you bankrupt. It's gonna cost you more than you have and leave you less than you started with. It will kill you from the inside out.

I once heard a story about Eskimos in Alaska who were having problems with wolves attacking their village, so they came up with a clever (although gruesome) plan. They took a sharp knife, dipped it in blood, and then let the blood freeze on the knife, which they then stuck into the ground with the blade facing up. The nearby wolves would smell the blood, make their way to the knife, and then lick it. They loved the taste of the blood, and it did not take long before they sliced their tongues on the knife and were licking their own blood. Eventually they would bleed to death, all the while licking the very thing that was killing them.

This is a tragic picture of humanity. We keep going back to the things that are killing us. We go back because the pleasure is so tempting. It is so tempting that we are willing to risk all that we have and all that we are on fleeting gratification. Like the Bible says, sin is pleasurable for a season. But like all seasons, pleasure does not last forever.

The only way out of this vicious cycle is to come out of the darkness and step into the light. We must acknowledge that we are sinners. We must confess, repent, and surrender our lives to Jesus. As long as we stay quiet about our sin, we will never experience the freedom that Jesus offers.

The sinful woman in Luke 7 is in a bad spot. She has been chewed up and spit out by the world. Her identity has been reduced to her sin. Yet she has learned something about Jesus, and she wants to learn more. Fortunately for her, Jesus' recurring message to people was simply, "Come." What do you do when the world has chewed you up and spit you out? You come to Jesus. No matter what you have done, no matter what has been done to you, come to Jesus.

If you're life is jacked up, come to Jesus.

If you're broken, come to Jesus.

If you're addicted, come to Jesus.

If you're afraid, come to Jesus.

If you're hiding, come to Jesus.

If you're ashamed, come to Jesus.

If you're guilty, come to Jesus.

This woman has a lot of baggage. She has made many mistakes, but it does not stop her from coming to Jesus. Remember it is not about what you are going through, it is about who you are going to.

People are going to look at what you have done, but God sees what you are going to do. The world will put its labels on you, but God is in the business of changing your name. Throughout the Bible, God was changing names:

- "Abram" went from being childless to being "Abraham," the father of a nation.
- "Jacob" went from deceiver to "Israel," God's chosen people.
- "Simon" went from a frightened and skittish disciple to "Peter," whom Jesus referred to as "the rock."
- "Saul" went from Christian-killer to "Paul," the greatest apostle ever.

This woman was simply known as a sinner, but Jesus had come to give her a new identity. Jesus is not careless. He is careful and welcoming. Maybe you feel like you have no identity. Maybe you feel like the nameless woman. Maybe you think your sin is your identity. I believe that God has a new name for you and that your ability to receive it is limited only by your willingness to go to him.

The world is strong, but God is stronger. Remember this: "Everyone born of God overcomes the world. This is the victory that has overcome the world, even our faith" (1 John 5:4).

In Christ, you can overcome the world.

Chapter Eleven

MOVING PAST
YOUR PAST

As she stood behind him at his feet weeping, she began
to wet his feet with her tears. Then she wiped them with
her hair, kissed them and poured perfume on them.
When the Pharisee who had invited him saw this, he said to
himself, "If this man were a prophet, he would know who is touching
him and what kind of woman she is—that she is a sinner."

LUKE 7:38–39

WHAT IS IT?

I love a good party with family, food, friends, fellowship, and fun. For DawnCheré's thirtieth birthday, I threw a big celebration. We had a DJ, great food, and some of our best friends dressed in all white. (We aren't celebrities, but sometimes it's fun to act as if we are.) We danced and laughed the night away.

After the party we drove home with a car full of presents for DawnCheré. Around 2 A.M., we sat on our balcony and she opened her gifts. One in particular caught our interest, an extremely heavy wooden crate. The card said it was from our friend Dave, who is an art lover and extremely creative. We couldn't wait to see what he had given DawnCheré.

We tore into the crate and discovered two big rock-like things. They each weighed about fifteen pounds. We had no idea what they were. They were cool, I guess, as much as two fifteen-pound rocks can be cool. But they were not especially beautiful. Clearly they were not sculptures. Nothing was written on them, so obviously Dave hadn't discovered the original Ten Commandments, which would have been a pretty dope gift. Were they miniature Stonehenge blocks? Maybe it was a joke and we were not getting the punch line. We concluded that Dave was way more artistic than we are and that his gift was too sophisticated for our understanding. I remember thanking Dave for the gift but having no idea what I was thanking him for.

For weeks those two rocks sat on the floor near our bed. We weren't sure where to put them because we didn't know their purpose. Sometime later Dave and I were talking on the phone and he asked, "How are you guys enjoying the bookends I got you?" At first I didn't know what he meant. Then it hit me. The two giant rocks! "Oh yeah, man!" I said. "We love those things! They look great in our house." When I got off the phone I grabbed the rocks, err, bookends, and put them on a shelf on either end of some books. They really did look great. They fit perfectly with the style of our place.

A gift that is misunderstood usually goes unused. If Dave had not clued me in, the bookends probably would have spent more weeks on our floor before being tossed in the garbage. It is hard to value what you do not comprehend.

I often meet Christians who have unwrapped God's gift of salvation but don't really understand what they have received. They're thankful, as much as they can be thankful for a gift they don't comprehend, but then they tuck it away and never experience the full power of the gospel.

For some people, though, the hardest part is accepting the gift.

JUST SAY THANK YOU

Some people do not know how to receive a compliment.

- "You look nice today."

+ "No, I just woke up and threw this on. My hair is a
  disaster."

+ "I love your shirt."
+ "This thing? It's super old. I didn't have time to iron
  the one I wanted to wear."

+ "You sounded great up there."
+ "I was flat on the second verse and my timing was off
  on the chorus."

You want to encourage people, but they refuse your encouragement. Maybe they don't want it or don't know how to receive
it. Or maybe they don't accept it because they don't believe it.

Many people treat God's gift of salvation this way. Some
don't think they need it. Some don't know how to receive it.
Others think it sounds too good to be true. You see, because
salvation is a gift it can only be received, not achieved through
human effort. The gospel is the good news—the gift that is
too good to be true but actually is true. There was nothing we
could do to earn it, so God gave it to us.

Here is how Paul explains it in Ephesians 2:8–9: "For it
is by grace you have been saved, through faith—and this is
not from yourselves, it is the gift of God—not by works, so
that no one can boast." We are saved by grace, through faith.
Salvation is from God. It has nothing to do with our efforts to
be good. It is not earned. It could not be earned. That is why
it is called a gift instead of a wage or a payment. After all, we
don't want God to pay us what we have earned. The only thing

we have earned is punishment. "For the wages of sin is death, but the gift of God is eternal life in Christ Jesus our Lord" (Romans 6:23).

Salvation is a gift from God. Unfortunately, many people accept this amazing truth but continue living as though their life depended on their works. But if good works could not save them, how could good works sustain them? The moment they start to live by works is the moment they begin to fall victim to a spirit of condemnation.

MINISTRY OF CONDEMNATION

Let's go back to the story about the sinful woman with no name in Luke 7. The Bible says that as she approached Jesus she fell on her knees and began to wash his feet with her tears. She opened a box made of alabaster and from it poured perfume onto Jesus' feet. Then she used her long hair to dry his feet.

What in the world was she doing? How would you react if a prostitute showed up uninvited to a party where you were the guest of honor, knelt down at your feet, busted open a marble box full of perfume, and then began scrubbing your feet using that perfume and her tears? And then she dried your feet with her hair. You would freak out, right? But Jesus did not freak out. Jesus knew exactly what this woman was doing.

In that day it was a sign of respect to anoint a person's head with oil or perfume. But this woman likely did not feel worthy of honoring Jesus that way, so she anointed his feet, the lowest part of the body. Luke tells us that she even kissed Jesus' feet, a sign of utmost humility and submission. The woman was expressing her tremendous gratitude to Jesus, most likely for the free gift of salvation. Her joy in Jesus' presence was so overwhelming that she couldn't stop crying. Her worship was loud and visible.

But right in the middle of her beautiful response to Jesus' grace, condemnation rears its ugly head:

> When the Pharisee who had invited him saw this, he said to himself, "If this man were a prophet, he would know who is touching him and what kind of woman she is—that she is a sinner."
>
> LUKE 7:39

The party's host, a Pharisee, was outraged that Jesus would allow this woman, probably a prostitute, to touch him. She was unclean. What was Jesus thinking, letting her touch him? As the Pharisee's response shows, it does not take much to reveal a spirit of condemnation. All you have to do is to start loving sinners. The moment you do, condemnation will rise up. We must not let the voice of the Pharisee be louder than the voice of the Savior. We must not let condemnation speak louder than grace.

DawnCheré and I were once in Santa Monica enjoying its Third Street Promenade, a beautiful street with great shopping and amazing restaurants. The road is closed to vehicles and in the center are all sorts of street performers. We sat there for hours watching and listening to some of the most talented, and not-so-talented, street performers from in and around Los Angeles.

One time, as I was walking through the Promenade, I noticed a large crowd, which is typical, especially when the performer is especially talented. But with this particular crowd something seemed a bit different and it caught my attention. As I drew closer I heard what sounded like preaching, but the man's voice was harsh, bitter, and angry. I pushed my way through the crowd and saw a man preaching his guts out. Fair enough. His topic was the judgment of God.

This is probably not the most popular topic you want to stand up in a crowd and shout about, but it certainly is not unbiblical. A few Old Testament prophets were pretty good at it. And this guy was railing against all sorts of sins—sexual sins, relational sins, nutritional sins, political sins, you name it. He was shouting angrily about all of them, and doing it in a way that was pretty offensive. I'm a fan of tough love, and I'm definitely a fan of biblical truth, but this seemed abusive. He had placed an open microphone in the center of the crowd and was inviting anyone to step up to the mic and challenge him. It was clear he just wanted people to tee him up so that he could launch into angry diatribes.

I watched as five or six persons walked up to the mic and asked him their questions. But the way he rebutted them with his "expert" answers embarrassed them. And he would cap it off by declaring that they were evil and doomed to spend eternity in hell. He also had a bunch of people with him who laughed and cheered and condemned anyone who dared challenge the preacher.

I watched for a few minutes, hurt and disappointed by what I saw. Were these really Christians? Did they really think this was what Jesus meant when he told us to preach the gospel? I was just about to leave when a young man walked up to the microphone. He politely introduced himself and said that he was gay. He then asked the preacher, "Does God hate me for being gay?"

The preacher responded as expected. He hurled vile and hateful insults at the young man, doing so in the name of God. He then demanded that the man repent or prepare to burn in hell. At that moment I'd had enough. I walked to the center of the crowd where the young man was standing, took the mic, and began preaching the gospel.

I told the preacher, "Having a burden for the lost doesn't mean that you are angry at the lost. Hating sin doesn't mean hating sinners." He muted the microphone, but I said, "I don't need a microphone." I looked at the crowd and said, "According to Romans, where sin abounds, grace abounds all the more. It's God's kindness that leads us to repentance. Today salvation is a free gift for you to receive. Repent and believe on the Lord Jesus Christ and you will be saved."

I wish I could say that a revival broke out then and there, that the Holy Spirit suddenly appeared like a rushing wind. But nothing extraordinary occurred, although a few folks in the crowd asked me more about Jesus and what I believed.

The proclamation of grace is intriguing and powerful. And to some people, such as the street preacher, it also seems to mean being offensive. Others can't accept that a just God would forgive people who don't deserve forgiveness. What they don't understand is that we don't deserve forgiveness. If we did, we wouldn't need it in the first place.

Sin, of course, is awful, and there is a time and place for calling it out. I'm not saying we should go soft on sin. I'm saying we should go bigger on grace. Condemnation is great at producing shame, guilt, and fear, and that is often how the Holy Spirit starts to bring us conviction for our sins. But none of these things are meant to be the basis for a healthy relationship with God or with anyone else. Relationships grow and mature based on honesty, trust, and love. And God wants us in that kind of relationship with him.

Have you ever cheated? Be honest. I cheated in my Spanish 2 class in high school. I did it when I had to take a test in detention. (I don't remember why I was in detention. Probably for cheating.) Ms. Cork was overseeing detention that day. You probably had a "Ms. Cork" at your school—dark and beady all-seeing eyes, sharp as a tack, not afraid to drop the hammer on a kid. Scary.

For this test I was supposed to write a Bible verse in Spanish. I had not studied for the test, so of course I did not know the verse, let alone in Spanish. So I did what any frontal-lobe-impaired teenager would do. Before entering the room I wrote the verse on one of my arms. I wore a jacket and slipped up the sleeve a little at a time to see the verse. But when I turned in my test I got caught. As I handed the test paper to Ms. Cork, my sleeve slid up just enough for her to notice something scribbled on my skin. "What's this, Mr. Wilkerson?" she asked. She caught me red-handed, or in this case, blue-armed.

Trying to weasel out of it, I replied, "I have written the Word on my body that I might not sin against God." What a shock. It didn't work. She turned my name in to the dean.

The next week, the dean called me to his office. I was terrified. He knew I cheated. I deserved to fail the class, and if I was caught cheating again I would be expelled. But instead of failing me, the dean talked to me. Even more shocking, he forgave me for what I had done. We talked for a while about school, about God, and about grace. He said that I shouldn't behave like that anymore. I knew he was right. I never cheated in Spanish 2 again.

Which is more fruitful, condemnation or forgiveness? Look at the world. Why are we in the mess that we are in? Is it because there is too much grace, forgiveness, and turning the other cheek? Or is it because there is too much guilt, vengeance, and retribution? Our world is a mess because of sin. God tells us that he will be the judge of all sin, but in our impatience, we insist on snatching the gavel from God's hand and doling out what we believe to be just, here and now, and the results speak for themselves.

Praise God that when we trust in Jesus, judgment does not fall on us. Paul tells us in Romans 8:1 that "there is now no condemnation for those who are in Christ Jesus."

We have all failed, but praise God for Jesus, in whom we are forgiven.

FORGIVEN

Here is one of my all-time favorite passages on God's forgiveness:

> When you were dead in your sins and in the uncircumcision of your flesh, God made you alive with Christ. He forgave us all

our sins, having canceled the charge of our legal indebtedness, which stood against us and condemned us; he has taken it away, nailing it to the cross. And having disarmed the powers and authorities, he made a public spectacle of them, triumphing over them by the cross.

COLOSSIANS 2:13–15

This passage begins with the fact that we were dead in our sins. We did not simply misbehave. We were dead. Yet God made us alive in Christ by canceling the written code (the Law) against us. It is important to understand what the Law is in order to truly appreciate the gift of salvation. It is hard to know why the gospel is good news if you don't know about the bad news.

In the garden of Eden, Adam and Eve had perfect intimacy with God. Nothing interfered with that kind of relationship. There was no immorality. There was no sin. Adam and Eve were naked and felt no shame. They walked with God in the cool of the day. Then Adam and Eve sinned against God by eating from the tree that he commanded them not to eat from—the Tree of the Knowledge of Good and Evil. The moment they did that, their perfect intimacy with God was tainted, just as a friendship is tainted when one friend abuses the trust of the other. Adam and Eve were banished from the garden, and an angel guarded the entrance with a flaming sword. This is a picture of what sin does. It separates us from God. Because of sin, mankind no longer had intimate access to God. Why? Because God is holy, blameless, righteous, and sin cannot be in his presence.

Incidentally, this is why we should never put sin into categories. I often hear Christians speak as though some sins are worse than others. I don't know whether that is true, but I know that God hates sin. All sin. Big or small. Whether it is socially acceptable or not, God hates sin.

We have a strange habit of comparing our sins to the sins of others. As long as we're doing better than our neighbors, we think we're good. But the fact is, our neighbors aren't the standard. God is. And the gap between people who are tainted by sin and a holy and righteous God is unfathomably huge. Sin separates us from God. It puts a huge chasm between us and God. The existence of the sin is what matters, not how big or how small we may think it is.

Trying to bridge that chasm in order to enter a relationship with God is like trying to jump to the moon. Our sin, no matter how small, separates us from God, and our good works, no matter how good, cannot even begin to bridge the chasm or come close to God's perfection.

When sin entered the world, life went bad quickly. As we discussed earlier, sin leads to more sin. It has a tendency to multiply exponentially. Thankfully, God eventually gave us the Law so that we might know how we ought to live, good and bad, right and wrong. The Law was first given to Moses on Mount Sinai in the form of the Ten Commandments, and it expanded afterward to include the Levitical law and many other laws. These were precise and specific rules that the priests and the people had to follow. Failure to obey them resulted in punishments of various sorts. Within this structure of rules and laws, a mechanism was established by which sins could be atoned once every year. In other words, there was a way for the Israelites to be reconciled with their perfect God.

ATONEMENT

Basically, here is how the process of atonement worked. You would bring some sort of animal, typically a young lamb, to the priest, who would slaughter and sacrifice the lamb to God. This resulted in the forgiveness of your sins. According to the Law, atonement of sins required the shedding of blood. Unfortunately, these animal sacrifices could only cover over, not remove, your sin. If you sinned again, the cover came off and your relationship with God was hindered once again. You would have to wait for the next Day of Atonement to perform the same ritual all over again.

But God's plan to reconcile people to himself did not stop there. Animal sacrifices were for a season, but not forever. Eventually, God sent his only Son, Jesus, on a mission to save sinners. Jesus came to do what we could never do and what animal sacrifices could never do. He fulfilled every part of the Law, wholly and completely. That is why he said that he came not to abolish the Law but to fulfill it. Perfectly.

But despite his perfect life, Jesus was sentenced to death on a cross. He did not die because of his own sin. He died because of ours, yours and mine. Jesus took our punishment. He took our death, the death we deserve as a consequence of our sin. He did not just die *for* you; he died *as* you. His perfect blood was shed as the ultimate and final atonement for your sins.

What is more, Jesus did not just come to cover over our sin. He came to remove it, to cancel it—past, present, and future sin, gone. No more animal sacrifices every year. The sacrifice of Jesus was the one sacrifice sufficient to atone for all sins of all time. This is why John the Baptist shouted when he saw Jesus, "Look, the Lamb of God, who takes away the sin of the world!" (John 1:29).

This is why the Bible speaks of Jesus as our High Priest when referring to what he accomplished on the cross.

> But when this priest had offered for all time one sacrifice for sins, he sat down at the right hand of God, and since that time he waits for his enemies to be made his footstool. For by one sacrifice he has made perfect forever those who are being made holy.
>
> HEBREWS 10:12–14

Notice that Jesus sat down at the right hand of the Father. Why is he sitting? Because his sacrificial work is finished. He completed the job. Jesus canceled the written code that was against us. He nailed it to the cross. He made a public spectacle of it. This was not some side deal between Jesus and God. This was the plan all along. Jesus, the Son of God, would willingly lay down his life as the ultimate sacrifice for our sin so that God could give us the gift of salvation. And it was done publicly. Jesus built a bridge out of the cross, and we can now cross the chasm and be reconciled to God our Father.

The cross is not just a symbol. It is a statement from heaven's throne that the penalty for sin has been paid. Forgiveness has been offered. Sin is canceled. Relationship with God has been restored. Eden is back open for business!

Still, if we aren't careful, we can waste this amazing salvation by allowing condemnation to rule us. The sinful woman with no name made her way to the feet of Jesus. Others in the room believed she wasn't worthy of even being in the room. They believed that her past disqualified her. But Jesus welcomed her.

I don't want you to live in the shame of condemnation. Jesus' sacrifice was so much greater than you may realize. Wherever you are today, I want to encourage you with three truths I have learned about God's grace.

1. There Is No Sin Too Big for God's Grace.

I don't care what you've done. If you will receive it, God's grace is more than enough:

> For I am convinced that neither death nor life, neither angels nor demons, neither the present nor the future, nor any powers, neither height nor depth, nor anything else in all creation, will be able to separate us from the love of God that is in Christ Jesus our Lord.
>
> ROMANS 8:38–39

Let's look at this. Death can't separate us from the love of God in Jesus. Neither can anything in life. Not even supernatural angels or demons. Nor can any power that exists. There is no place too high or too deep for God's love to reach you. Nothing, nothing in all of creation can separate you from God's love in Jesus Christ. I think that about covers it.

Look at Jesus instead of at your sin. He doesn't condemn you. He convicts you, sure, and that conviction comes from the Holy Spirit to remind you of Jesus. Condemnation says, "You've gone wrong. You have failed. It's over for you." Conviction says, "You've gone wrong. You have failed. Confess your sin, and turn from your failure and toward the cross of Jesus Christ. He is faithful and just and will forgive you of your sins and purify you from all unrighteousness."

Do you see the difference? Condemnation says that you're heading down a bad road and there's no turning around. Conviction say that you're heading down a bad road but Jesus can help you turn around and get back on the right road.

Whenever I have moments of weakness, the Holy Spirit reminds me of Jesus. Even when I am weak, he is still strong. Here's what Paul said about it:

> But [Jesus] said to me, "My grace is sufficient for you, for my power is made perfect in weakness." Therefore I will boast all the more gladly about my weaknesses, so that Christ's power may rest on me.
>
> 2 CORINTHIANS 12:9

Conviction is all about drawing you to Jesus. It's a warning signal that something isn't right and needs to change. Christ has paid the price to make the change possible, and the Holy Spirit provides us the strength to make the change take place. Paul, writing to the church at Ephesus, describes the process this way:

> As for you, you were dead in your transgressions and sins, in which you used to live when you followed the ways of this world

and of the ruler of the kingdom of the air, the spirit who is now at work in those who are disobedient. All of us also lived among them at one time, gratifying the cravings of our flesh and following its desires and thoughts. Like the rest, we were by nature deserving of wrath. But because of his great love for us, God, who is rich in mercy, made us alive with Christ even when we were dead in transgressions—it is by grace you have been saved. And God raised us up with Christ and seated us with him in the heavenly realms in Christ Jesus, in order that in the coming ages he might show the incomparable riches of his grace, expressed in his kindness to us in Christ Jesus. For it is by grace you have been saved, through faith—and this is not from yourselves, it is the gift of God—not by works, so that no one can boast.

EPHESIANS 2:1–9

God convicts us, and God, by Jesus, saves us. Thank God for conviction, forgiveness, and new life in Christ!

2. You Are Not What You Have Done.
You Are Who God Says You Are.

Look, I don't know you. You may have done some bad stuff, like really bad, stuff that I might be frightened by, or that you wouldn't tell anyone, or that you're ashamed of to this day. But listen, I've done some bad stuff, too, that I don't want you to know about, stuff that makes me cringe to think about, stuff that I would give almost anything to go back and undo. But here's the great news: We don't have to be defined by that stuff. God made us. Let's let him define us. This is why it's so vital that we ingrain God's Word into our lives. We need to hear his Word over the world's word.

We might feel useless, but God says that we were fearfully and wonderfully made. That means that he planned us and took care to make us just the way he wanted. The Bible says that we are the righteousness of God through Christ Jesus. What if we could grab hold of that truth? We are the righteousness of God through Christ Jesus. What a thought! Little ol' Richie Wilkerson, fallen, sinful, dead in his trespasses, is the righteousness of God because of Jesus Christ. This is something we ought to proclaim over our lives every single day. We are the righteousness of God through Jesus Christ. I challenge you to speak this truth even during times of failure and weakness, because the truth of the statement stands firm; it doesn't change based upon your behavior. It is grounded in Jesus' finished work on the cross.

The other day I was talking to my two-year-old niece, Carolina Lee. I asked her, "Carolina, do you know that you are the prettiest girl in the world?"

"Yes."

"Carolina, do you know that you are the smartest girl in the world?"

"Yes."

"Carolina, do you know that you are the best singer in the world?"

"Yes."

Then I asked her, "How do you know all these things, Carolina?" She looked me in the eye and confidently replied, "My daddy told me so."

If you are a believer, your heavenly Daddy is speaking to you. What might happen in your life if you started listening to what he is saying? What if you started believing what he says about how much he cares for you, about your future, about the hope he has for you, about the fact that he is working everything in the world together for your good? My friend, your future is bright. How do I know? Because Jeremiah 29:11 says, "'For I know the plans I have for you,' declares the LORD, 'plans to prosper you and not to harm you, plans to give you hope and a future.'"

3. You Can't Change Your Past, but You Can Write Your Future.

Some people spend their whole lives trying to change the past, to make up for the mistakes they made, the birthdays they missed, the abuse they inflicted. Sometimes they even try to change the story so that they won't remember its being as bad as it was. But for all their efforts, the past does not change. What is done is done. Trying to change the past is futile. And the fact is, if you're always looking backward it is hard to move ahead. It's tough to drive a car forward while staring into the rearview mirror.

When a circus elephant is young, its trainer puts a chain around its ankle. The chain is tied to a stake in the ground to keep the young elephant from wandering off. What's interesting is that when the elephant grows into an adult, the trainer still uses the same chain and stake, which is now not nearly strong enough to hold back an adult elephant. So if the adult tried to escape, it could. Yet, it doesn't try to escape because it has been trained to believe that it can't break that chain.

The fact is, it's not the chain holding the adult elephant back. It's the elephant's belief that holds it back. In the same way, as a forgiven believer in Christ, you may believe that your past is holding you back. But the truth is that your past has no power over you. It's only your belief that is keeping you down. Choose to move forward in the power of Christ, and that chain cannot hold you.

Paul illustrates this point so powerfully. Early in his life, Paul was a Pharisee named Saul, and he was really good at being a Pharisee. He was zealous for the Jewish faith. He knew the Law inside and out, and he wasn't fond of lawbreakers. That's putting it lightly. Actually, Saul's full-time job was to hunt down Christians and punish them for breaking the Law. Sometimes that meant having them put to death.

But the resurrected Jesus got to Saul. He appeared to Saul when Saul was on the road to Damascus to deal with the Christians there. That meeting with Jesus changed Saul's life. From that point forward Saul was known as "Paul," and Paul's impact for the kingdom of God is virtually unrivaled. Paul did not allow his despicable past to keep him from achieving all that God had destined him to do. Paul was the primary early evangelist to the Gentiles (non-Jews). Many consider him the greatest of all the apostles. His letters account for nearly half of the New Testament. I love how Paul describes his journey forward. He says he forgets what is behind and strains toward what is ahead.

> Not that I have already obtained all this, or have already arrived at my goal, but I press on to take hold of that for which Christ Jesus took hold of me. Brothers and sisters, I do

not consider myself yet to have taken hold of it. But one thing
I do: Forgetting what is behind and straining toward what is
ahead, I press on toward the goal to win the prize for which
God has called me heavenward in Christ Jesus.

PHILIPPIANS 3:12–14

This passage is a great reminder that sometimes you just
have to

- Quit focusing on what you did in the past.
- Quit focusing on what you didn't do.
- Quit allowing yesterday to dictate today.
- Quit letting the enemy tell you who you are.

The devil brings up your past because he is running out of
new material. Every time he brings up your past, you need to
remind him of his future. You can't change your past, but Jesus
can change your future.

Chapter Twelve

THE PARABLE

Jesus answered him, "Simon, I have something to tell you."
"Tell me, teacher," he said.
"Two people owed money to a certain moneylender. One
owed him five hundred denarii, and the other fifty. Neither
of them had the money to pay him back, so he forgave the
debts of both. Now which of them will love him more?"
Simon replied, "I suppose the one who had the bigger debt forgiven."
"You have judged correctly," Jesus said.
Then he turned toward the woman and said to Simon, "Do you
see this woman? I came into your house. You did not give me any
water for my feet, but she wet my feet with her tears and wiped them
with her hair. You did not give me a kiss, but this woman, from
the time I entered, has not stopped kissing my feet. You did not put
oil on my head, but she has poured perfume on my feet. Therefore,
I tell you, her many sins have been forgiven—as her great love
has shown. But whoever has been forgiven little loves little."
Then Jesus said to her, "Your sins are forgiven."

The other guests began to say among themselves,
"Who is this who even forgives sins?"
Jesus said to the woman, "Your faith has saved you; go in peace."

LUKE 7:40–50

Position Produces Performance

My parents are firm believers in the value of hard work. My dad made sure that I worked somewhere every summer when I was in high school. Most summers I made minimum wage helping the janitorial team at my dad's church. Honestly, it wasn't that bad, except for the whole cleaning the toilets part. I worked with cool people. I was constantly affirmed, and I never worried that I was going to lose my position. I was the preacher's kid, after all.

Before my senior year of college I worked for a successful and wealthy man. The only catch was that this man was a little erratic. He was temperamental, and it was impossible to know what mood he would be in on any given day. When he was in a good mood he would hire people left and right. When he was in a bad mood he would fire people quicker than Donald Trump. Some days he was kind and other days he was mean. You just never knew. The littlest thing could make him fly off the handle. As a result, everyone was afraid of losing his or her job. It seemed like every day the conversation at work focused on the chances of not having a job tomorrow.

If you are constantly afraid of losing your job, you may work diligently but you won't work passionately. Chances are, your heart won't be in it. I never really bought in to what I did at that job, and I certainly did not try to shine. I never even gave my honest opinions because I thought that if I did I might lose my job. The boss wasn't looking for leaders. He was looking for followers. Actually, he was looking for yes-men. It was not a great place to work.

In most of life we usually don't get a position unless we can perform, and if we stop performing we often lose that position. People try hard so that they can keep their positions. But this is not how the kingdom of God works. In the kingdom of God your position does not depend on your performance. Your position was purchased by Christ.

The moment you receive salvation your position changes from sinner to child of God. Nothing can change that. And rather than performing to earn or keep your position, your position results in performance. You are not living *for* a blessing. Once you are in the family of God, you are living *from* a blessing. Let me try to explain.

The apostle Paul was often referring to his position in Christ and reminding others that they were "in Christ" (2 Corinthians 5:17). He also said that "through him," Christ, we can do all things (Philippians 4:13). You can't do all things by your own strength, but if you are in Christ nothing is impossible.

Colossians 3:3 says, "For you died, and your life is now hidden with Christ in God." We are wrapped up in the Son of God. When God looks at us he sees Christ. That's what it means to be "in Christ." If you have been hidden in Christ, quit getting lost in yourself.

When we trust in the world instead of in Christ, we tend

to focus on our performance in the world. Am I successful enough, rich enough, smart enough? Do I dress well enough? And as we have seen already, when we measure ourselves by such self-imposed standards, we never get where we think we ought to be. It's a futile pursuit. We're never enough. We're bankrupt. But when we put our trust in Jesus, we are reminded that our performance does not dictate our position. His performance has already secured our position, in him. And since we already have that position, we are truly free to perform.

It has been said that you never really know who you are until you know whose you are. In Christ, you are a son or a daughter of God. You are a joint heir with Jesus. That means that you, little ol' you, a sinner saved by the grace of God, will one day inherit what Jesus inherits. What a thought! What amazing grace! Once you understand whose you are, then you are free to do what you were redeemed to do.

There is a common criticism, and fear, about preaching this grace. If you preach grace, people might end up doing whatever they want and live according to the world's standards and desires. They will just do whatever feels good and believe that God will forgive them in the morning. In other words, they will not obey God. They will not perform in the way I have been taking about here.

I understand this fear about preaching grace, but I am not talking about what some theologians call cheap grace. The more we grasp just how wide and long and high and deep the love of Christ is, the more we will understand what he has done for us, what it truly cost him. As that dawns on us, the more we are willing to live for him. Grace, properly understood, does not result in a license to sin. Grace results in gratitude.

The Bible tells us that Jesus was the "last Adam" (1 Corinthians 15:45). The first Adam was in the garden of Eden, and he and Eve introduced sin into the world. Jesus is called the last Adam because, instead of introducing sin into the world, he introduced God's grace. If the first Adam's actions brought a curse upon the world, how much more do the actions of the last Adam, Jesus Christ, bring a blessing by removing sin and replacing it with righteousness? Paul points this out:

> For just as through the disobedience of the one man the many were made sinners, so also through the obedience of the one man the many will be made righteous.
>
> ROMANS 5:19

Friend, we need to realize that Jesus paid all of our debt. The more we celebrate this, the more inclined we will be to walk in righteousness.

In our final story in Luke 7, the woman's actions are a picture of the beautiful exchange of salvation. Walking in unannounced, she falls down at Jesus' feet and starts worshiping him. Her tears wet his feet and she dries them with her hair. She uses perfume to anoint Jesus' feet. Imperfection meets perfection. Brokenness encounters wholeness. Grace results in gratitude.

Yet, as we have seen, in the middle of this tender moment, the Pharisee thinks that Jesus doesn't know that this is a sinful woman who is touching him. Jesus' response is phenomenal. He doesn't scold the Pharisee and thus embarrass his host. Nor does he cast the woman out or even give a knowing nod and gracefully steer her away. No, in true Jesus fashion, he stays right in the tension and teaches yet another truth about God's love and grace. And he does it by telling a parable.

STORY TIME

"SIMON," JESUS SAID, "I HAVE SOMETHING TO TELL you": "Two people owed money to a certain money-lender. One owed him five hundred denarii, and the other fifty. Neither of them had the money to pay him back, so he forgave the debts of both. Now which of them will love him more?"

LUKE 7:40–42

I love how Jesus answers our complicated questions with simple answers. In this case he uses a story to give a simple, but profound, answer. It's a fictional story, but if you think about it, it's the story of us all. Jesus says that two men owed money to a lender. Let's say one man owed $500, the other owed $50. Neither could pay it back to the lender. Both were bankrupt. In America these men could probably file for Chapter 7 bankruptcy, sell what they own, and be done with it. But in Jesus' day bankruptcy wasn't so simple. Often debtors who couldn't pay what they owed became slaves in order to work off their debts.

The truth is that all of us are like those men. We are all spiritually bankrupt. We owe what we cannot pay. We trusted in ourselves for peace and happiness. We trusted in others. We trusted in religion. We trusted in the world. And we still came up short. We may have felt temporarily satisfied, but ultimately we were unfulfilled. What's worse, we ended up enslaved to the things that we thought would give us joy.

In a typical bankruptcy proceeding, the debtor makes every effort to settle his debts. He pays what he can, and hopefully the lender will accept the payment in satisfaction of the debt. But in Jesus' parable the creditor forgives both of the debts. He cancels them completely. No settlement. No "pay what you can." Forgiven. Paid in full. As Jesus finishes this story he asks Simon the Pharisee a question:

> "Now which of them will love him more?"
>
> Simon replied, "I suppose the one who had the bigger debt forgiven."
>
> "You have judged correctly," Jesus said.
>
> LUKE 7:42–43

Simon the Pharisee knew the Law. He had all of the information. He knew the rules and regulations. He knew what was required of him, and he had done his best. But what did his knowledge and expertise lead to? In this story, little more than apathy and arrogance. Jesus points out the difference between the Pharisee and the sinful woman, and it certainly was not what the Pharisee expected to hear.

> Do you see this woman? I came into your house. You did not give me any water for my feet, but she wet my feet with

her tears and wiped them with her hair. You did not give me a kiss, but this woman, from the time I entered, has not stopped kissing my feet. You did not put oil on my head, but she has poured perfume on my feet. Therefore, I tell you, her many sins have been forgiven—as her great love has shown. But whoever has been forgiven little loves little.

LUKE 7:44–47

It was customary in those times for a host to greet a guest with a kiss and to offer him water to wash his feet. But Simon does neither. In contrast, as soon as the sinful woman saw Jesus she washed his feet with her tears and kissed his feet repeatedly out of respect and submission. She even poured costly perfume on them. Jesus explains that she did all of this not because she knew a theology of forgiveness but because she had encountered forgiveness in person.

Jesus says to the Pharisee that people who have been forgiven little love little, but people who have been forgiven much love much. It is not the awareness that I am a sinner that leads me to worship Jesus. It is the awareness that I am forgiven.

The woman is not worshiping because she is sorry (which she is). She is worshiping because she has been set free of her debt, which has been paid in full by Jesus. Because her debt has been paid, she wants only to be with the one who paid it. She hasn't merely been saved; she has been given new life in Christ, a new identity and a new purpose. She did not have to change her lifestyle first, in order to earn Jesus' grace. But now that she has received Jesus' grace, she wants to do exactly that. God's grace results in gratitude, and gratitude combined with God's power leads to changed life.

PROSTITUTE TURNED QUEEN

One of my favorite books is *Classic Christianity*, by Bob George. The book includes a powerful illustration about how the motivation of the believer changes as we encounter the fullness of God's grace.

> Let me share an illustration. Let's imagine that a king made a decree in his land that there would be a blanket pardon extended to all prostitutes. Would that be good news to you if you were a prostitute? Of course it would. No longer would you have to live in hiding, fearing the sheriff. No longer would you have a criminal record; all past offenses are wiped off the books. So the pardon would definitely be good news. But would it be any motivation at all for you to change your lifestyle? No, not a bit.
>
> But let's go a little further with our illustration. Let's say that not only is a blanket pardon extended to all who have practiced prostitution, but the king has asked you, in particular, to become his bride. What happens when a prostitute marries a king? She becomes a queen. Now would you have a reason for a change of lifestyle? Absolutely. It doesn't take a genius to realize that the lifestyle of a queen is several levels superior to that of a prostitute. No woman in her right mind would go back to her previous life.
>
> As long as a half-gospel continues to be taught, we are going to continue producing Christians who are very thankful that they will not be judged for their sins, but who have no significant self-motivation to change their behavior. That's

why so many leaders have to use the hammer of the law and suffocating peer pressure to keep their people in line.

But what is the church called in the New Testament? The bride of Christ! The gospel message is in effect a marriage proposal. And just as the prostitute became a queen by marrying the king, guilty sinners have become sons of God by becoming identified with Christ. It is that relationship and our new identity that becomes our motivation, and it is motivation that comes from within.

SHE WORSHIPED

The woman worshiped Jesus. It was emotional. It was messy. It was probably loud. She was in the presence of the man who saw past her past and forgave all of her sins, past, present, and future. She was elated. I bet she thought something like, "Thank God I'm not where I used to be. I should be dead. I should be in jail. I should be pregnant. I should be divorced. Oh, but he paid my debt! I have a reason to worship him!"

Friend, we worship at the level that we believe we have been forgiven. When you realize you have been forgiven much, you love much and you worship much.

The more we meditate on Jesus' finished work, the more we fall in love with him. Preaching grace does not lead to wild behavior. Not according to Jesus. Preaching grace leads to worship of the Savior. Our love and devotion grows when we focus on the Savior, not on ourselves.

I have never met a Christian who exaggerated God's love toward him. It's impossible. God bridged an infinite gap with his infinite love. The more we focus our eyes on God's amazing grace, the more we grow in our faith. In fact, you might define spiritual growth as the process of becoming more Savior-conscience than sin-conscience. Jesus forgives the woman based upon her faith. Yet even faith is the result of grace. The Bible tells us that we are dead in our sin, and a dead person can't have faith. Even faith, then, is a gift from God.

Ultimately, we need to know that our sin is not stronger than our Savior.

The Savior is greater than our sin.

The Savior is greater than our mistake.

The Savior is greater than our guilt.

The Savior is greater than our shortcoming.

Jesus is our Savior. He is our forgiveness. The Bible is full of stories of his love and mercy. And I want you to know that the Bible is not just a book about what God did in the past. It is a biography of a living God, and that God is at work today in the world. What God did in the past, he can do today. God has always been in the business of saving people.

THREE TYPES OF PEOPLE

My wife and I have been together since we were seventeen. Now we're in our thirties. We want to have kids, but we don't have any yet. We're working on it. (Practice makes perfect, I hear.) And just now we have a different schedule than most people our age. Our nights tend to drag on into the wee hours of the morning. We usually start with dinner and just go where the night leads us.

Now, DawnCheré is amazing in many ways, but she's not the homemaker type. She's a great cook, but she doesn't enjoy it. You aren't going to find her in the kitchen wearing an apron baking cakes and pies in the oven. And I'm definitely not a cook. So dinner usually means going to a restaurant. Honestly, I love going to restaurants. I'm definitely a food guy. I love all sorts of cuisines. Since we eat out so much, we have picked up on some patterns in the dining world. For example, when it comes to paying for the bill, there are three basic types of people.

- THE MOOCHER. This type includes those who conveniently leave their wallets at home. As soon as the bill arrives they start looking nervous. They lean over and pat their backside. They reach inside their jacket. They pat their shirt pocket, then their pants pocket. They look left and right and finally look up sheepishly and say, "Man, I'm so sorry. I totally forgot my money. Can you get this one?" I've always wondered how people can honestly forget their money when they're going out to eat. Did they think the restaurant might be running a special "all-you-can-eat-for-free" night?

- THE MATHEMATICIAN. This type is more annoying than the first. These are the people who pull out calculators the second the bill arrives. Their goal is to divide up the check perfectly. They want everyone to pay exactly what they owe. They have charts and graphs and spreadsheets. "Okay, you owe $1.25 for the diet Coke and $7.99 for the chips and salsa." Look, I appreciate what they're trying to do. They're just trying to make it fair. But if there are a lot of friends having dinner together, who has time for all that Texas Instruments' graphing calculator stuff?

- THE MAN. This is my favorite. When the bill comes this guy just puts his credit card down and handles it without saying a word. He simply pays the bill. He's the man.

I'm sure you know who the man is in your group. In my world it's my dad. I always know that when I go out to eat with my dad he is going to pay the bill. No questions asked. No awkward, "You can get it next time." No silly back and forth, "No, let me," or, "No, please, I insist." When the check comes he just handles it. (Call me spoiled if you like. That's probably fair.)

I've noticed, too, that when my dad asks me to go to lunch, I don't ever say, "No, Dad! I'm not going. I hate going with you! You always pay the bill! I'm over it! This has got to stop!" No way. On the contrary, I get excited when Dad invites me to lunch. I can't wait to go. It's more like, "Hey Dad, let's go to Ruth's Chris Steak House!" The fact that he buys doesn't push me away; it draws me closer to him. It makes me want to be around him even more.

Friend, this whole book is a declaration that Jesus has paid your bill. The check came, and you owed more than you have. In fact, you have nothing. You are completely bankrupt. But thankfully, Jesus is the Man. He took care of your debt. Once you are aware of what he paid, it doesn't lead you away from him, it leads you straight to him.

My prayer for you is that after seeing what Jesus has done for you, you will run toward him with everything in you. Don't just give him part of your life. Give him all you've got. After all, he gave it to you in the first place. He desires to have a real, intimate relationship with you. He is not mad at you. He is madly in love with you. He has paid every debt you ever owed and ever will. And when you let Jesus have *all* of your life and let him be your king, you will no longer be building on sand but on the immovable, unshakeable, eternal Rock.

ACKNOWLEDGMENTS

THANK YOU TO MY WIFE, DAWNCHERE. YOUR ENCOURagement and belief in me keeps me going. Our friendship is forever ever.

I'm thankful to my parents, Rich and Robyn Wilkerson, for always speaking to my potential. Having you as parents is the key to so much of the good in my life.

And thanks also to the following: My brothers and sisters for loving me. The people of Trinity Church and Vous Church for teaching me so much about what Jesus looks like. David Hicks for working with me daily and helping make the words look so beautiful; this project could not have happened without you. Esther for telling me we had a chance. Thomas Nelson and all the wonderful people there for making the book a reality. Soho House for keeping the library open all night for me.

Lastly, thank you to Jesus Christ, my lord and savior. You are my heart's desire. You are the only firm foundation. This book is by you, for you, and all about you. Thank you!!!!!!!

ABOUT THE AUTHOR

 RICH WILKERSON, JR., AND HIS WIFE, DawnCheré, are the founders of the VOUS Church in Miami and the annual VOUS Conference on South Beach at the historic Fillmore Theater. Rich is also the host of the weekly talk show *Top3* on JUCE TV, which features popular Christian personalities and roundtable discussion on current news. An internationally recognized speaker, Rich has logged more than two million air miles preaching the gospel to hundreds of thousands of people around the globe. www.vouschurch.com